/ARCHITE

/ARCHITECTURE 02

the riba awards/tony chapman

BATSFORD

BRITISH LIBRARY CATALOGUING IN PUBLICATION
A CIP RECORD FOR THIS BOOK IS AVAILABLE FROM THE BRITISH LIBRARY

PUBLISHED BY B T BATSFORD, A member of **Chrysalis** Books plc
64 BREWERY ROAD, LONDON N7 9NT
WWW.BATSFORD.COM
EDITOR ROSA AINLEY
DESIGNER CLAUDIA SCHENK

FIRST PUBLISHED 2002
COPYRIGHT © 2002 THE ROYAL INSTITUTE OF BRITISH ARCHITECTS

ISBN 0 7134 8793 3

PRINTED IN GREAT BRITAIN BY TFW PRINTERS, LONDON

FOR A COPY OF THE BATSFORD CATALOGUE OR INFORMATION
ON SPECIAL QUANTITY ORDERS OF BATSFORD BOOKS PLEASE
CONTACT US ON 020 7697 3000 OR SALES@CHRYSALISBOOKS.CO.UK

CONTENTS

JUDGING THE STIRLING PRIZE 2002

I sometimes wonder why we go to the lengths we do when all William Hill has to do to pick a winner is look at a few pictures and chat up a couple of journalists. Mind you, time and again they get it wrong and we get it right. You see, the favourite seldom wins. Maybe this year will be different.

Organising schedules for busy successful people makes you realise why they're successful. They pack ridiculous amounts into their days. And this lot have agreed to give up three of them, when they could be designing buildings or clothes, writing books or running the architectural world, in the cases of, respectively, RIBA President Paul Hyett and Foreign Office architect Farshid Moussavi; Wayne Hemingway, who used to be Red or Dead but now is neither but still designs everything from clothes to houses in Gateshead; writer and inventor of the Orange Prize for Fiction Kate Mosse; and Paul Finch, Channel 4's man in the white mack last year and the only survivor from the 2001 panel.

Paul is in charge for the first leg as I've avoided the early flight by dint of being in Gateshead already, spending a day in meetings with BALTIC, the amazing new centre for contemporary art, designed in his nappies by Dominic Williams, where we're staging the presentation and dinner. I've also been doing press, TV and radio interviews. They're immensely proud of their bridge in Gateshead and still prouder that it's on this year's Stirling Prize shortlist. But is it a building, they want to know? For me, a building's anything that gets built, and they're happy to be convinced. I only hope the judges agree: one journalist threatened us all with a lynching if the bridge didn't win.

I've seen it half a dozen times already but for some of the judges it's their first sight of this year's hot favourite and they're as knocked out by its grace and beauty as I was the first time. John Johnson, the Gateshead engineer/client behind the project, has arranged for the bridge to be raised in our honour, though Paul Hyett has to wait several minutes for a number of people in wheelchairs crossing it to clear before pressing the button. As we watch the whole structure slowly tilt, we wonder if John's aim is to stop us getting back to Newcastle. It is, after all, Gateshead's bridge; they paid for it (along with you and I through our lottery tickets). The attitude on the north bank seems to be, if Gateshead people want to get to Newcastle, let 'em pay! Why would Newcastle people want to get to Gateshead? The answer is increasingly obvious: BALTIC. People are crossing the bridge in their droves to see it (a quarter of a million – the first year's target – in the first three months) and soon there'll be Foster's Music Centre too, rapidly taking shape just upstream. And then there's the bridge, a destination in its own right as well as a link. That's what bridges do: they bring people together, whatever their differences. But seldom so elegantly as this. The two places are coming together too in the joint bid for European City of Culture in 2008: another hot favourite …

The bridge comes down in time for us to cross north to pick up a cab to catch the Edinburgh train. (They have the same problem with cabs here as in London: 'South of the river? You've got to be joking, pet.') It's good to have a Scottish building on the list again, the first since Benson + Forsyth's Museum of Scotland in 1999 when we presented the prize there, and they came second … Their latest offering is drawing us across the Irish Sea to Dublin later in the day but first we go to see Malcolm Fraser's Dance Base, a building that does its best to get into Edinburgh Castle without paying, so high does it clamber up Castle Rock. The neat way it does so was enough to encourage those of us who judged it earlier for the ADAPT Trust Access Award to give it first prize. But we're less concerned about Part M of the Building Regs and more about how it works for everyone. Malcolm Fraser is a man who knows his city and loves it. This is a building that is thoroughly at home here, unlike certain other recent additions to the city that look as if they have been flown in ready-made. Dance Base seems to grow out of the rock.

There are four very different dance studios, two of which – one old and one new –

frame dramatic views of the castle through their roofs. The judges all love the lightweight metal roof structure, exposed when the ceiling was removed from the studio overlooking the Grassmarket, but wonder if it's right to give points for something that already existed. But there are points aplenty for the neat way the spaces link effortlessly together. Also for cheek: the artistic director has not only turned up in a pair of Red or Dead shoes, she also presents Wayne with a kitsch doll.

Wayne and Kate keep disappearing to top up on retro heaven in the 1960s clothes shops that seem to abound here, returning laden with bags of booty. Wayne 's even found time to sign autographs. One shop owner said he was going to stick up a sign stating 'Wayne Hemingway was here, Kate Moss wasn't'. The rest of us are getting stuck into the excellent menu of a strangely deserted fish restaurant nearby. It's remarkable there's time for lunch in today's hectic schedule, but it's good to have a chance to discuss the two buildings we've seen already: is it right to separate, however loosely, bikes from people on the bridge? And is it right to accept toys from competitors?

Dublin, our next stop (and it's still only day one), attracted more entries this year than any other town save London, but sadly achieved only two RIBA Awards. And one of those is technically outside the city: Fingal Council Offices, Bucholz McEvoy's first building, with the help of BDP Dublin. That's an object lesson to local authorities everywhere. We're here to meet Raymond Keaveney, Director of the National Gallery of Ireland.

'Wow,' goes up the chorus as we enter its cathedral-like atrium. More than one of the judges is more impressed than they expected to be. Paul Finch remarks on the way in which, in common with a number of follow-up projects, the architects have developed the best and restrained the excesses of their earlier work. There's scarcely an artwork in sight to distract the judges – usually a problem in judging any exhibition space – as they're between shows. The resulting pure white spaces appeal particularly to the architects among us who tend to hold the view that paintings, like people, get in the way of architecture. There are no people either, as they've stayed open late especially for us.

We enjoy poking around its nooks and crannies as the Channel 4 cameras watch and listen. In the first two years they covered the Stirling Prize, they went everywhere with us. This year, they've been more selective: they've chosen here, the school and Germany (choices presumably not made on grounds of cost then). Afterwards the Director takes us off to a pub for a pint of Guinness, a gesture you wouldn't expect from all directors of national museums. There Raymond fills us in on a few of the problems they had, not only with the planners who insisted they hang on to a couple of buildings on the site ('Just build around them would you?'), but also with their own chief fundraiser, one Charlie Haughey, disgraced ex-Taoiseach whom they had to sideline quietly; and then there were the builders who were called out on strike for nine months in mid-construction. All the more remarkable an achievement.

Monday's the easy day: three more buildings but all in London and the south east of England. Jerry, our usual driver on such jaunts, is a gambling man and a good barometer. Two years ago he correctly picked Peckham Library. Last year, like everyone else except the judges, he went for Eden. This year, he's spreading his bet between the bridge and our first stop today, Hampden Gurney School, a unique high-rise school by Building Design Partnership, just off the Edgware Road. Ms Chua, the Head Teacher, guides us from the basement playground, hemmed in by the new housing that is funding the whole project, up through six circular floors of classrooms and semi-open play decks to a roof protected by a Hopkins' Lord's Mound Stand-style white canvas tent, where a class of six-year-olds is enjoying an alfresco lesson, oblivious of the cameras. They've seen it all before, there's been so much media interest already that they're not impressed. Besides, they're part of the multi-channel generation, so cameras do not hold the interest they did in my day.

Next up is the Richard Rogers Partnership Lloyd's Register of Shipping, possibly the practice's most challenging brief to date. Farshid calls the planners the architectural police, there to see that architects behave themselves and don't frighten the horses. From street level there's nothing to frighten the most nervous of passing nags, as all you see are the carefully restored façades. But stand back and the slender glass towers peer at you over the top; dive through the hole punched in the front and you're in a tranquil courtyard where a fountain plays and you can see how the towers elegantly meet the ground. Lloyd's Register, with its services colour-coded in the Rogers' house style, is a distant cousin of Lloyd's of London and it does what it says on the tin: it's the Architects' Registration Board for shipping, settings standards for the way ships are built.

Client Peter Hayward has shown round more juries than he could shake a stick at – four for RIBA awards alone – and though he's beginning to feel like an estate agent, his pride in the achievement is undiminished. Maybe this is an architect's building, with plenty of detailing to marvel at, but there's plenty too for the lay person to admire: the restoration of the sumptuous Victorian interiors (one totally relocated from third floor to first); the way old meets new in an inner hall; and the exciting but effortless Finnish lifts that whisk you skywards (though their voices could do with redubbing in better English). Surprisingly the Rogers Partnership have never won the Stirling Prize – could this be their year?

Our charabanc awaits to whisk us through the Surrey and Sussex countryside, via the less than bucolic Wandsworth one-way system. And thanks to a sandwich lunch en route, we're ahead of schedule when we arrive at the Weald and Downland Open Air Museum near Chichester. Director Richard Harris (not *that* Richard Harris) trained at the Architectural Association but never got round to qualifying as an architect. Instead he's dedicated his professional life to saving threatened buildings, restoring and re-erecting them in these beautiful surroundings. What they needed was a decent place to carry out the conservation work and one where visitors could watch them doing so.

Enter Ted Cullinan, who has long been fascinated by Ted Happold's lightweight structures. The Downland Gridshell is a vast hangar of a place, like an upturned boat (appropriately enough, as many of its craftsmen were boatbuilders). In practice, it's more like a dry dock, only they work on buildings rather than ships. The structure is hand crafted from laths of green oak – French, since you ask but if we're talking sustainable sources, Normandy is nearer than Northumberland. Each length is narrow enough to bend into the honeycomb forms that give strength to the soaring, undulating structure that surrounds you as you enter the awesome space.

The whole was draped like a blanket over a scaffold then tugged into place over a six-week period. The result is a building unique to this country and a prototype for other applications as diverse as sheds and pool houses. Richard says that the teams of carpenters behaved as well as cathedral builders: no copies of *The Sun*, no swearing and definitely no striking. Perhaps that's why it came in on time and within its modest budget of £1.6 million. The only quibble of the Awards Group jury – that although it is fully accessible from one end, there is only a flight of steps at the other – is now being addressed, as a new wheelchair route is beginning to snake its way through the trees. For the second or third time, the Stirling judges agree this is the one to beat.

Unanimity soon breaks down on the M4: should we stick in this queue, or turn off through Hayes? My credibility is in tatters an hour and a half later when we still haven't reached Hammersmith after I opted for sticking with the M4 and Wayne and Paul Hyett are running late for their evening appointments. Someone else had better do the navigating tomorrow; I'm doing the driving anyway.

We're all back at Heathrow before the larks have even thought of breaking wind and on our way to Düsseldorf. As I drive them across the plains of north-west Germany, Paul Hyett wants to give the wind turbines that dot the landscape a prize. Shame they weren't designed by a British architect. The village of Lette is our destination and Ernsting's Service Centre. The staff here used to work in cramped Portakabins, so their transfer to the coolest and emptiest of Chipperfield buildings must be quite a shock. The landscaping has been completed since my visit in April with other members of the Awards Group (meaning I have to reshoot the video I'm making for the evening of the presentation). Art and nature have turned the piles of earth into swards of green, softening the hard lines of the concrete and glass pavilions. Similar contrasts abound inside: where rails of cheap, brightly coloured clothes designed on the premises counterpoint the minimalist architecture. There's even a company shop where they try out the latest lines on the employees. Commerce is neatly balanced by art. These paternalistic employers apparently stage concerts and plan to hang art in the vast and all-but-empty entrance space, though there's little evidence of either on our visit.

Channel 4's cameras follow us round. British Airways lost their tripod so the camerawoman's shoulder must be aching by the time the judges have finished a long and, I suspect, eminently cuttable discussion on cost and value in architecture. In the Calatrava-designed canteen over lunch of North German delicacies like pork, potato dumplings and red cabbage, the judges discuss their preferences, causing our host Herr Weckert to scuttle off to the smoking area. As the crew are on a break, they also discuss how much they're prepared to reveal when they're back. Afterwards, the judges are picked off one by one by producer Mike Lerner. Back on the road, they compare notes on what they were asked and what they said. 'I told them architects were a load of pillocks,' says Wayne. 'Didn't really,' he adds. We'll have to wait till October to find out.

The people mover resembles a mobile call centre, with all five judges on the phone at once. Even Kate, who had earlier marvelled at the amount of business architects seem to have to do every hour of the day and night, has caught the bug. And I'm left to read the map and try to catch up the ten minutes we're behind or fail to get us to the airport in time to catch the flight. We'll all be together again at BALTIC in three weeks' time. In the meantime I have a dinner and presentation to organise, videos to edit and this bloody book to write. All they have to do is come up with a winner. They will of course, but it's never been closer, whatever William Hill says.

the stirling prize

THE STIRLING PRIZE 2002

The RIBA Stirling Prize, now in its seventh year, is sponsored once more by *The Architects' Journal* and is awarded to the architects of the building thought to be the most significant of the year for the evolution of architecture and the built environment. It is the UK's most prestigious architectural prize. The winners receive a cheque for £20,000 and a trophy which they hold for one year.

The prize is named after the architect Sir James Stirling (1926–92), one of the most important British architects of his generation and a progressive thinker and designer throughout his career. He is best known for his Leicester University Engineering Building (1959–63), the Staatsgallerie in Stuttgart (1977–84) and his posthumous Number One Poultry building in London. His former partner Michael Wilford won the 1997 Stirling Prize for the jointly designed Stuttgart Music School, and this year won an RIBA Award for the building which completed Stirling's masterplan for Braun at Melsungen in Germany. Seven RIBA Award-winning buildings were shortlisted for the Stirling Prize, following second visits by members of the RIBA Awards Group.

THE 2002 SHORTLIST: Dance Base, Edinburgh, **MALCOLM FRASER ARCHITECTS**; Downland Gridshell, Weald and Downland Open Air Museum, **EDWARD CULLINAN ARCHITECTS**; Ernsting's Service Centre, Coesfeld-Lette, Germany, **DAVID CHIPPERFIELD ARCHITECTS**; Gateshead Millennium Bridge, **WILKINSON EYRE ARCHITECTS**; Hampden Gurney School, London, **BUILDING DESIGN PARTNERSHIP**; Lloyd's Register of Shipping, London, **RICHARD ROGERS PARTNERSHIP**; Millennium Wing, National Gallery of Ireland, Dublin, **BENSON + FORSYTH**.

The winner of the 2002 RIBA Stirling Prize in association with *The Architects' Journal* is the Gateshead Millennium Bridge by Wilkinson Eyre Architects.

GATESHEAD MILLENNIUM BRIDGE

In 1997 Wilkinson Eyre won a competition to design a new foot- and cycle-crossing of the Tyne to link Gateshead with Newcastle. It was to play a pivotal role in the regeneration of Gateshead, with Ellis Williams' BALTIC centre for contemporary art and Foster and Partners' Music Centre, tying this new arts hub to Newcastle's recently developed quayside.

The brief called for a footbridge which met the ground on either riverbank; others, because of the Tyne's steep gorge, do so further inland. This was likely to mean a steep gradient (or steps) if there was to be sufficient clearance even for small craft, making it inaccessible to wheelchair users or any but the fittest cyclists. Wilkinson Eyre instead proposed a curved deck to reduce the gradient. This in turn suggested a solution to the other part of the brief: a mechanism for allowing the occasional passage of bigger traffic, for example, the tall ships. The Swing Bridge, some way up stream, is a low-level solution, but that pivots from an island; the Victorian Tyne Bridge solves the problem of obstruction to shipping by towering high above the water. In its lowered position, Wilkinson Eyre's bridge allows the same clearance as the Swing Bridge and when raised gives a 25-metre clearance, the same as the massive Tyne Bridge. And it does so in spectacular fashion.

The idea is eminently simple: a pair of arches – one is the deck and the other supports it. Both pivot around their common springing point allowing shipping to pass beneath. As the whole bridge tilts, it undergoes a metamorphosis into a grand arch in an operation that evokes the slow opening of a huge eye. Side on, when raised, it takes on the shape of a human heart. Powerful images both.

The design is a subtle mix of the robust and the delicate and contracts effectively with the vast bulk of BALTIC which it abuts. The bridge spans 105 metres between two caissons. An all-glass pavilion encloses the plant and hydraulics on the south bank. The parabolic arch has a kite-shaped cross section that tapers in plan and elevation. The pedestrian route is slightly raised above the cycle way and there is intermittent screening.

Wilkinson Eyre Architects

GATESHEAD MILLENNIUM BRIDGE

Seats give the bridge a sense of place as well as purpose. The structure was built in sections in Bolton, assembled at Wallsend then shipped upstream and dropped into place on its concrete abutments by a giant crane to within a tolerance of 1 millimetre. One false move could have wiped out the thousands watching the procedure on either bank.

The wonder of this project speaks for itself. It started with the vision of the clients and their decision to appoint Wilkinson Eyre Architects, in partnership with the experienced bridge engineers Gifford's. Every aspect of the bridge, from conception and detail through to execution, is simple and incredibly elegant.

In choosing the bridge as this year's winner, the Stirling judges described it as architecture and engineering in close harmony. Architecture, they said, is about the enclosure of space and this does just that because it moves. Its shape changes depending on where you are standing: a blinking eye, cupped hands or a human heart. At night it looks like a sparkler describing all these shapes and more in the sky.

Few pieces of architecture have had such a powerful social effect, providing a powerful stimulus to regeneration, helping to end the traditional enmity between Gateshead and Newcastle and bringing them together in a joint bid for City of Culture status in 2008. It is, the judges concluded, a new icon. This is the one piece of new architecture that will be remembered by people this year. We see now that Wilkinson's Eyre's was the obvious solution: it was just that no one had ever thought of it before.

CLIENT Gateshead Council
STRUCTURAL ENGINEER Gifford & Partners
M&E ENGINEER Gifford & Partners
LIGHTING CONSULTANT Jonathan Speirs & Associates

CONTRACTOR Harbour & General
CONTRACT VALUE £17.7 million
PHOTOGRAPHY Graeme Peacock/ Doug Hall

Wilkinson Eyre Architects

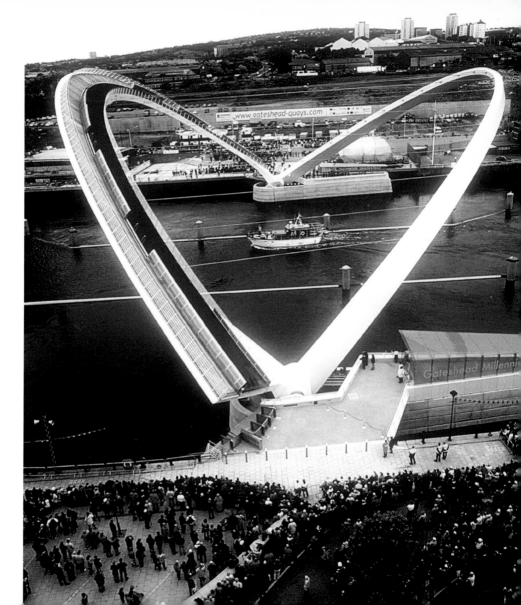

DANCE BASE, EDINBURGH

This is one of the most complex projects to win an award in recent years and, as such, presented a remarkable challenge in terms of access. Constructed on the lower slopes of the volcanic crag topped by Edinburgh Castle, behind and above existing buildings, Dance Base provides a wonderful group of four dance studios, as well as changing rooms, administrative offices and social facilities. Few planning authorities would have been so bold as to risk such a striking a new building in this context.

Arranged over a succession of four levels – a combination of lifts, stairs and ramps providing easy access – the building magically exploits the topography of the site. One ramp leads up from the generous reception space, hugging an illuminated old stone wall, to a second foyer where the high quality of the concrete is exposed.

Each studio is unique. One, converted from an existing building and overlooking the Grassmarket, is a simple space with a lightweight steel trussed roof and a single rooflight punched through to offer a dramatic view of the castle. A second, like a giant conservatory, has an almost entirely glazed roof. The castle's looming presence seems to fill this space. This studio, which opens off the foyer, is used by Dance Base's integrated creative movement programme for dancers with disabilities, often working with their carers. The third has a beautiful floating steel roof suspended above its perimeter walls. And the last, the most restrained and the most elegant, is enclosed by a powerful in-situ concrete structure. At the top of the building the space opens out on to a series of terraces, decks and gardens, colonising the hillside and providing a wonderful amenity in this dense urban location and further views of castle and city.

The Stirling judges said, 'This is a place that makes you want to dance, even if you can't. It is an inspirational building whose glass roofs and skylights frame the constantly changing Scottish skies every bit as much as they frame dramatic views of the castle. But as well as providing four very different spaces, using different materials, for the dancers

Malcolm Fraser Architects

DANCE BASE, EDINBURGH

to work in, the Dance Base is equally generous in its provision of social spaces, not least in the outside places which are a wonderful surprise. A dancer would not feel as if they were coming to work here, rather they would want rather to linger and swap gossip and tips. It is also, appropriately, a very tactile building: you want to run your hand along the smoothness of the handrails and compare it with the roughness of the walls. All in all, the architects have given the clients far more than they ever thought they could have, which is the mark of good architecture.'

Also winner of the 2002 ADAPT Trust Access Award, see pages 62–63.

STRUCTURAL ENGINEER Cundall Johnston & Partners
M&E ENGINEER K J Tait
QS Morham & Brotchie Partnership
THEATRE DESIGNER Andrew Storer Designs

ACOUSTICS New Acoustics
LIGHTING CONSULTANT Jonathan Speirs
CONTRACTOR HBG
CONTRACT VALUE £5 million
PHOTOGRAPHY Keith Hunter Photography

Malcolm Fraser Architects

DOWNLAND GRIDSHELL
WEALD AND DOWNLAND OPEN AIR MUSEUM, CHICHESTER

All museums are about discovery and the best ones, like the Weald and Downland Museum, share not only the results but also the process of discovery with their visitors. This admirable museum presents the history of vernacular architecture in the south-east in a hugely enjoyable way and on a lovely site. It has been responsible for saving many historic buildings threatened by development and has formed important collections of materials and artefacts. Under the directorships of the late Chris Zeuner and, latterly, Richard Harris, the museum has also been a potent source for the teaching of craft building techniques.

So the context is as extraordinary as the building itself: the world's first permanent timber gridshell building. Rather than construct a fake barn to house the storage and workshop space it needed, the museum decided to commission a new work of architecture that would reflect the relevance of the vernacular tradition today. It is really two buildings, one on top of the other. The conservation workshop where buildings are brought, worked on and returned to site, is 50 metres long and sits above a concrete plinth that houses the offices and storage. The structure is like a fine musical instrument, using a variety of different woods best suited to purpose: local or Normandy oak, ash, Douglas fir and western red cedar. The laths of timber of which the Gridshell is constructed are used here in a highly innovative way though there are antecedents outside the construction industry, in the design of World War II aircraft. The computer-aided design process, carried out in close collaboration with engineers Buro Happold, was realised by exceptional craftsmen. This is a scheme where brief, process, construction, materials and detail all combine to produce a whole which is much more than the sum of the parts. The Heritage Lottery Fund, part financiers of the project, now use it as a model procurement method.

The regional jury felt it was ground-breaking and lovable; an extraordinary building and a joy to visit. They concluded, 'It is a major work by a practice which has enriched the architectural culture of Britain over four decades. The building is inclusive, accessible,

Edward Cullinan Architects

DOWNLAND GRIDSHELL

innovative, (truly) sustainable and beautiful.' And as the critic Nic Pople wrote in *The RIBA Journal*: 'For architects cynical about what can presently be achieved, this is an object lesson in daring to dream.'

The Stirling judges were just as enthusiastic about this unexpected building: a beautifully crafted timber structure among the living trees. It shows, they said, that good design makes a difference and demonstrates what can happen when a gifted architect remains closely involved throughout the whole process, right down to the detailing. That said, one of the lay judges thought this was the kind of thing people feel they could have a go at in their own gardens. Its potential as a prototype for buildings as diverse as swimming pools and industrial sheds impressed them most. They considered it the kind of space you could throw anything at and it would enhance the activity. The museum has just appointed Joe Thompson, a local craftsman, to use the space to work on both the Downland's and his own projects; to be in effect an exhibit in his own right.

There was what Richard Harris described to the judges as 'a planning moment': a loss of confidence by the planners which caused them to ask for the building to be drawn back among the trees. But that is after all the natural habitat of a timber building and of the other buildings, many half-timbered, that make up this remarkable museum. The Gridshell is a thing of beauty inside and out and a tribute to all who worked on it.
Also shortlisted for The RIBA Journal Sustainability Award.

CLIENT Weald and Downland Open Air Museum
STRUCTURAL ENGINEER Buro Happold
M&E ENGINEER Buro Happold
QS Boxall Sayer

CONTRACTOR E A Chiverton Limited/ Green Oak Carpentry Company
CONTRACT VALUE £1.6 million
PHOTOGRAPHY Stuart Keegan

Edward Cullinan Architects

ERNSTING'S SERVICE CENTRE
COESFELD-LETTE, GERMANY

This represents another successful German commission for David Chipperfield. Ernsting are a down-market clothing retailer and the vivid examples of their range provide a bizarre contrast with the coolness of the building containing them. An enthusiast for modernism, the client has already had Bruno Reichlin, Fabio Reinhart and Santiago Calatrava design parts of the site for him. Calatrava designed a set of unique and beautiful steel doors for the distribution depot next door and a signature bridge that went nowhere until Chipperfield completed this building. This is clearly a man who collects good buildings like other well-off people collect cars or paintings. Although these were all good pieces of architecture in their own right, the site as a whole did not have a clear identity. The challenge laid down in this competition brief was not only to add another fine piece of architecture, but to create a sense of campus and to unify the spaces between existing and new buildings.

Chipperfield's winning entry proposed a pavilion of open and flexible office spaces arranged round a series of gardens, courtyards and an atrium. The atrium is a generous space where employees can meet over coffee, for conferences and seminars, where exhibitions can be hung and these benign employers can indulge their employees with concerts and displays of art. (The space is dominated by an enormous woodcut, which was damaged when hidden from the Nazis and later restored by Herr Ernsting's son.)

Until the staff moved into their new offices, they were housed in warehouse containers. Their new offices are transparent and humane, taking full advantage of the parkland setting. Although open plan, each workspace has its own balcony, its own link with the outside world. Elegant, automatic canvas blinds afford protection from the sun. This is a standard of office provision almost unthinkable in the UK. There are just over 100 people working in the new building, with provision for 200, and it feels eerily empty – maybe because another employer might have squeezed another 200 people in.

At first sight, this building appears more like a gallery or maybe an airport before the

David Chipperfield Architects

ERNSTING'S SERVICE CENTRE

franchises move in. And it has resonances of the golden era of high-quality corporate headquarters. Closer inspection reveals that it rises way above the norm. What is really impressive is the variety of spaces, views and connections that the architects have drawn out of an apparently simple plan, based on a repeated module. The skill has been in exploiting a luxurious budget without becoming indulgent. A remarkably generous set of spaces, with high ceilings, wide corridors and open loggias is the result.

The mastery is in the deployment of those elements and their control through the established virtues of clarity and attention to proportion. The building has a timeless quality; it is calm and calming. Particularly impressive are the controlled framing of views to the outside and the handling of light. All of this with a limited palette of materials that could have been unforgiving but here is almost soft and entirely human in its handling.

The Stirling judges praised it for its tremendous maturity and control. All the judges enjoyed the almost surreal juxtaposition of the client's populist clothing range with the high art of the architecture – good architecture should lift the spirits and in this Chipperfield has succeeded supremely well. It is the exact opposite of the clothing sweatshop and an inspiration to all who work there. So it is also good business: the building's calming effect, far from proving soporific, has actually led to an increase in productivity. To raise the spirits and improve the bottom line is no mean achievement for an architect.

CLIENT Ernsting
STRUCTURAL ENGINEERS Jane Wernick Associates with Arup Düsseldorf
M&E ENGINEER PGH, Dormagen
LANDSCAPE ARCHITECT Wirtz

International, Schoten
CONTRACTOR E Heitkamp GmbH
CONTRACT VALUE £11.5 million
PHOTOGRAPHY exterior, Edmund Sumner/interior, Christian Richters

David Chipperfield Architects

HAMPDEN GURNEY CHURCH OF ENGLAND PRIMARY SCHOOL
NUTFORD PLACE, LONDON W1

This is a scheme which turns school design on its head – and turns heads too. Hampden Gurney is an innovative multistorey primary school developed on an inner-city site formerly occupied by one- and two-storey buildings which had reached the end of their useful life. The school prides itself on its high academic standards and had sought, for a number of years, to improve its premises in order to provide its pupils with a school worthy of the twenty-first century. The solution came through a deal with the contractor Jarvis to redevelop two parts of the site for housing. When the Stirling judges visited, phase one was complete and noisy work for phase two was going on. This has not been an easy journey for the school, which has had to be kept open throughout construction. The housing does crowd the basement playground, but then this is an inner-city school and its design more than compensates.

The new building makes the school the cornerpiece of a recreated Marylebone city block, looking out towards the constant activity of the Edgware Road nearby. With the residential buildings to the rear and side, it forms an internal courtyard which is used for organised games for all ages. Glazed doors to the hall-cum-chapel peel back to create one circular indoor–outdoor space.

The six levels of the building make it a landmark in the neighbourhood and the 'vertical school' offers opportunities for safe weatherproof play in the open-air play decks and the prospect of open-air classrooms on warm days, with good north light in the teaching areas. Not only do children 'move up' the school metaphorically as they get older, but at Hampden Gurney they literally 'move up' in terms of floors of classroom occupation.

This could be described as the world's first suspension school. It has a steel frame crowned with a heavy arched truss at fourth-floor level; macalloy bars support the bridge steels in the lightwell, transferring the loads to the truss overhead and enabling the communal hall to be free of columns. The outer envelope is brick, chosen to be sympathetic to

Building Design Partnership

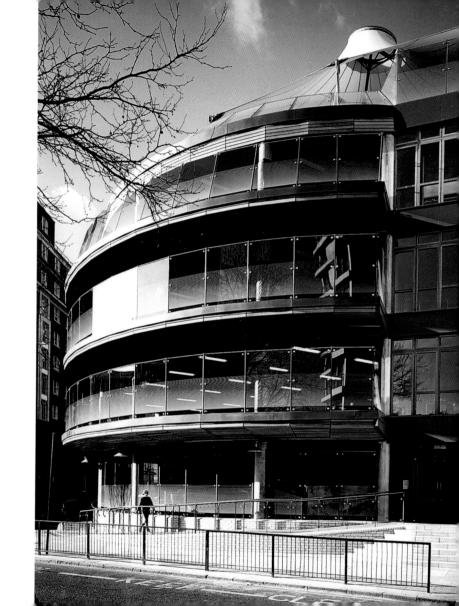

the surrounding London stock brick buildings, while the curve of the play decks is formed by the 1.9 metre-high glass balustrading. A tensile roof springs from the steel truss, protecting the lightwell below and creating threshold spaces to work in on the roof play area. The covered playground on each level is shared between three classrooms, which allow play even when it is raining. There is a central atrium that brings light into the centre of the building and the overall organisation and environment feels safe and spacious.

The Stirling judges said they were moved to see the children's pride in their school in their faces. They appeared to be all the more appreciative of the generous provision of personal space because so few of them enjoyed such luxury in their homes. The judges were also impressed by the ambition of both client and architect and the way in which they have combined to find a creative solution to the problem of building affordable and well-designed schools in our cities. They have thrown the Hampshire County Architects inspired rulebook, laudable and inspirational though that has been when applied in appropriate contexts, out of a sixth-floor window and invented a new form. There may be precedents – the Victorian neo-gothic block and, latterly, Elder and Cannon's St Aloysius' Primary School in Glasgow – but it has not been done in the last 100 years in England. Hopefully this will be a prototype that will develop and mature in other hands and on other sites. Now for hospitals ...

CLIENT Hampden Gurney School
STRUCTURAL ENGINEER Building
Design Partnership
M&E ENGINEER Building Design Partnership
QS Building Design Partnership

CONTRACTOR Jarvis Construction
(UK) Ltd
CONTRACT VALUE £6 million
PHOTOGRAPHY Martine Hamilton Knight

Building Design Partnership

LLOYD'S REGISTER OF SHIPPING
FENCHURCH STREET, LONDON EC3

Good architecture often comes out of adversity and conflict. Basil Spence's Coventry Cathedral used the blackened shell of the firebombed medieval church as its inspiration and its pivot. RRP's new headquarters for Lloyd's Register of Shipping does much the same thing, combining the reworking of existing listed properties around the perimeter of the site with the insertion of an uncompromising new structure within. The project develops, refines and updates the trademark elemental construction language seen within Lloyd's nearby sister building to create a vibrant and animated presence within the City.

From street level the new building is generally concealed by the surrounding original buildings, its presence only revealed through an abstract louvred elevation to Fenchurch Street and glimpses across a small courtyard behind the retained corner pub to the main entrance. From longer views though, the new building can be clearly seen, its slender glass lift towers growing out of the site to soar above the enclosing stone façades – and most of the City of London.

The project rationalises the original disparate mix of buildings and levels into a coherent group linked at first-floor level. The need to retain an original churchyard within the site has been turned to advantage, creating an intimate entrance court, a calm space within the bustle of the city, through which workers pass to reach the new building or gather around the elegant fountain to chat or, inevitably, smoke a cigarette.

A steep, wide stairway (with lift alternative) climbs out of the courtyard to a revolving glass door, giving on to a generous reception area which is currently shared by Lloyd's Register and its tenants who occupy the upper floors, but the landlords are creating themselves a parallel entrance and foyer. The first of two full-height atria rises above the main entrance space allowing visitors to see the different levels within the building. On an operational level, the atria break up what could have been a bland expanse of office floor plates, allowing daylight to filter through to the workstations and creating a means of

STIRLING PRIZE SHORTLIST

Richard Rogers Partnership

mediating temperature differences between the outside and the offices. Energy efficiency is explored throughout the design, which incorporates mechanisms such as chilled beams and louvred façade systems to respond to external environmental conditions, minimise running costs and create comfortable working environments.

The quality of the working environment is continued through the attention to detail in both the new building and the refurbishment of the original premises. The best elements of the old buildings have been retained and meticulously restored. These include the meeting room that was moved in its entirety from third floor to first and a lavish board room, its furnishings intact, where an exquisite frieze was discovered under an undistinguished painting. The articulation of the new elements creates an identity and character within the offices and emphasises the kit-like method of construction that the access difficulties to this confined site necessitated.

The Stirling judges described this as a thoroughly exciting building in an extraordinarily difficult context: hi-tech guts dropped into an existing urban landscape, with all the services pared down into fragile elements. They particularly enjoyed the urban space of the courtyard – formerly a churchyard – which gives the building a popular outdoor foyer. They thought this the practice's best work for some time and commended the way in which it overcomes planning and site constraints to add a very special piece of architecture to the City.

CLIENT Lloyd's Register of Shipping
STRUCTURAL ENGINEER Anthony Hunt Associates
M&E ENGINEER Arup
QS AYH Partnership

CONTRACTOR Sir Robert McAlpine & Sons Ltd
CONTRACT VALUE £70 million
PHOTOGRAPHY Katsuhisa Kida

Richard Rogers Partnership

MILLENNIUM WING, NATIONAL GALLERY OF IRELAND
DUBLIN

In the Millennium Wing of the National Gallery of Ireland in Dublin, Benson + Forsyth have taken their experience of working on the Museum of Scotland and refined and honed it to produce these breathtaking gallery spaces. It is a glowing cathedral of a place which brings joy to the hearts of the Dubliners it serves, succeeding in combining loftiness with intimacy, gravity with playfulness, and theatricality with calmness. It triumphantly fulfils the client's brief that it 'should be dignified and expressive of its time and its function', and that 'the interior should be legible to visitors and a delight to experience.'

The Millennium Wing was the result of an international competition won in 1996 and finally opened to the public in 2002, after many setbacks including the loss of its main fundraiser, disgraced ex-Prime Minister Charles Haughey; a reduction in gallery space; and a planning requirement to include within the footprint a Georgian and a Regency building. Nonetheless, the completed gallery, far from feeling like a compromise, has a sense of inevitability about it. The two existing structures now face one another across the restaurant. The Regency one has been particularly cleverly integrated. Though it appears at first glance to be a mere façade, it is very much three dimensional, containing a beautiful domed meeting room behind its tricksy barn door.

The new galleries are linked to the existing ones at right angles, and have their own street frontage. This façade is treated as a play of shifting planes of Portland stone, between which the inside of the gallery can be glimpsed. This relationship with the city continues throughout the building, culminating at roof level from which the familiar landmarks of Dublin can be seen. Sadly, funding did not allow for a lift to this level so, because it is not accessible to wheelchair users, the roof is off-limits for all but staff. Hopefully the next stage of development will rectify this.

Inside, although the vast vertical circulation spaces are asymmetrical and sometimes dizzying, the galleries themselves are ordered and calm, allowing visitors to con-

Benson + Forsyth

GALLERY OF IRELAND

centrate on the art they have come to see. Curatorial demands are not so stringent as to exclude natural daylight, so there are very few areas that are artificially lit, and this adds to the accessibility of the experience. What gives this building its very special timeless quality is its consistency, which extends through into its (at times risky) detailing. A special mention should be made of its use throughout of a light stone-coloured self-finished plaster that seems to absorb light and radiate it back again.

Although the façade on Lincoln Place contains all the clues about what to expect inside, nothing quite prepares you for the majesty of the soaring space within and the Stirling judges were audibly surprised and delighted. It is a bold but effective stroke to give up so much of the building's volume to an atrium with scarcely an artwork in sight but it succeeds in setting the tone for the building as a whole, with its references to Rome and the Scottish baronial. The inevitable commercialism of a modern gallery is all here – bookshop to the left, restaurant to the right – but they speak the same language because the clients insisted they were done by Benson + Forsyth themselves.

The Stirling jury enjoyed the remarkable level of control, for all the exuberance of the building. Architecture is about the manipulation of three-dimensional space – four if you include the exhibits – and here the architects have built a modern cathedral to art. The judges enjoyed themselves here: one of them was so impressed by the entrance space, he turned round and came in again just to experience that thrill once more. Dubliners can count themselves lucky they can enjoy this on a regular basis.

STRUCTURAL ENGINEER O'Connor Sutton Cronin
M&E ENGINEER Oscar Faber
QS Rogerson Reddan Associates

CONTRACTOR Michael McNamara and Co
CONTRACT VALUE £10.7 million
PHOTOGRAPHY Hélène Binet

Benson + Forsyth

special awards

THE STEPHEN LAWRENCE PRIZE

The Stephen Lawrence Prize, sponsored by the Marco Goldschmied Foundation, was set up in 1998 to draw attention to the kind of creativity architects have to display when working on low budgets. It is awarded, with a cheque for £5000, to the architect of an RIBA Award-winning building costing less than £200,000. The prize commemorates Stephen Lawrence, the black teenager who was planning to become an architect when he was murdered in South London in 1993, and supports the charitable trust set up in his name.

The Marco Goldschmied Foundation, established by RIBA past president Marco Goldschmied, supports the Stephen Lawrence Trust and a number of construction and property industry charities.

THE 2002 SHORTLIST: Basement Flat, Edinburgh, **RICHARD MURPHY ARCHITECTS**; Wycoller Visitor Centre, **HAKES ASSOCIATES**; The Cardboard Building, Westcliff-on-Sea, **COTTRELL + VERMEULEN ARCHITECTURE**; Quaker Barns, Norwich, **HUDSON FEATHERSTONE**; Bandstand, De la Warr Pavilion, Bexhill, **NIALL McLAUGHLIN ARCHITECTS**; Sorrel House, Bosham Hoe, **FOGGO ASSOCIATES WITH DAVID THOMAS**; Fairhazel Gardens, London NW6, **SCAMPTON & BARNETT**.

The winner of the 2002 Stephen Lawrence Prize is The Cardboard Building, Westborough Primary School, Westcliff-on-Sea by Cottrell + Vermeulen Architecture.

An exceptionally interesting and, literally, multifaceted project, The Cardboard Building combines the vision of the schools' staff and governors with the tenacity of the architect and engineer to research the structural aspects of the project and obtain the necessary permissions from a sceptical local authority. The project demanded that the designers obtain free materials from manufacturers in order to realise what would otherwise have been unaffordable. The building is made almost entirely from recycled materials, which may be recycled again in future. The building is not the most advanced folded structure ever developed but moves the science of cardboard structure forward significantly, within the limited resources available. It also acts as a continuous learning experience for successive cohorts of children both in terms of the strength and economy of folded structures and the sustainable issues which the building demonstrates. A brave attempt on a shoestring budget, embodying the truth that 'necessity is the mother of invention'.

THE CARDBOARD BUILDING, WESTBOROUGH PRIMARY SCHOOL
WESTCLIFF-ON-SEA

Westborough's head teacher is an exemplary client. Over 13 years she has cajoled and wrung from the county, the DfES and other sources, money to repair and replace outworn buildings and upgrade playground areas, introducing landscaped areas with the active participation of the children. This large primary school with some 900 pupils from 3–11 years serves the immediate depressing Edwardian streets and provides the focus of infor- mal out-of-school play, and a stimulating teaching environment for the young pupils.

The Cardboard Building, funded through the DETR/DTLR's Partners in Innovation programme, is the latest of several buildings constructed with a minimum budget and is innovatory and unusual in concept and implementation. It uses 90 per cent recycled mate- rials and the intention is that the same percentage will be recyclable at the end of its life.

The form of the building was inspired by origami and the intrinsic strength of folded paper. The children were involved from the outset, collecting card, doing designs which the architects tried out, as well as their own ideas, in a series of folded paper models. Walls and roof are made of load-bearing cardboard panels which are also naturally insu- lating. Cardboard tubes are used for pillars and the palisade walls.

This is a building of high ambition realised through the drive and tenacity of client and architect. It takes practical sustainability as a core value, and has stimulated and engaged its users from concept to execution in a way that would make major corpora- tions envious.

Also winner of The RIBA Journal Sustainability Award and shortlisted for the RIBA Client of the Year.

THE STEPHEN LAWRENCE PRIZE

STRUCTURAL ENGINEER Buro Happold
M&E ENGINEER Buro Happold
QS Buro Happold

CONTRACTOR C G Franklin Building Ltd
CONTRACT VALUE £177,157
PHOTOGRAPHY Peter Grant Photography

Cottrell + Vermeulen Architecture

THE CROWN ESTATE
CONSERVATION AWARD

The Crown Estate Conservation Award is made to the architects of the best work of conservation which demonstrates successful restoration and/or adaptation of an architecturally significant building. It carries a prize of £5000.

The Crown Estate manages a large and diverse portfolio of land and buildings across the UK. One of its primary concerns is to make historic buildings suitable to the needs of today's users.

THE 2002 SHORTLIST: Centre for Contemporary Arts, Glasgow, **PAGE & PARK ARCHITECT**s; Stirling Tolbooth, **RICHARD MURPHY ARCHITECTS WITH SIMPSON AND BROWN;** Great Hall, Belfast, **CONSARC CONSERVATION;** Sorrel House, Bosham Hoe, **FOGGO ASSOCIATES WITH DAVID THOMAS;** Tate Britain Centenary Development, **JOHN MILLER & PARTNERS.**

The winner of the 2002 Crown Estate Conservation Awards is the Stirling Tolbooth with Richard Murphy Architects and Simpson Brown Architects jointly cited as winners.

Murphy's insertions are as dramatic as they are well-judged. He has taken the old courtroom and placed the main performance space here, dramatically cutting away one end of the room to increase seating. He has also enclosed the courtyard with a glass wall which floods the entire building with light.

The work of Murphy and Simpson Brown Architects strips back and reveals aspects of the building's history in an understated way. The judges were particularly impressed with the way in which the team had taken a sadly neglected and under-used yet histori-cally important building and made it a focal part of the life of the town.

STIRLING TOLBOOTH

This is a truly ingenious project: a much needed venue for the making and performance of music in a surprisingly poor part of the town, despite its proximity to the castle. A whole succession of new arts facilities – performance spaces, foyers, rehearsal rooms, cafe, restaurant and recording studio – have been squeezed meticulously into the shell of this group of late medieval buildings.

The result is an extraordinary sequence of spaces at the heart of which are a winding steel staircase and a glazed lift. Each turn of the – very industrial, very Murphy – stair reveals a new component of the building; some new spaces, some existing rooms carefully protected and revealed. Here the meticulous hand of conservation architects Simpson & Brown is revealed. The existing buildings formed a U-shape, of which the original courtroom formed the lower part. Murphy has placed the main performance space here, dramatically cutting away one end of the room. The interventions fill up the remainder of the U-shaped courtyard, providing for the foyer and the building's circulation system. The new space is enclosed with a glass wall which floods the entire building with light.

Despite the extraordinary complexity, every detail here is beautifully resolved. Fundamental to the scheme is some very ambitious structural and mechanical engineering. And while the integrity of the original building is carefully protected, the new elements appear with a flourish on the exterior, adding a new landmark to the city's silhouette. Also shortlisted for the ADAPT Trust Access Award.

CLIENT Stirling Council
STRUCTURAL ENGINEER David Narro Associates
M&E ENGINEER Buro Happold
QS Morham & Brotchie

ACOUSTICS Sandy Brown Associates
CONTRACTOR Hunter & Clark
CONTRACT VALUE £4 million
PHOTOGRAPHY Alan Forbes/RMA

Richard Murphy Architects with Simpson & Brown Architects

AJ FIRST BUILDING AWARD

The AJ First Building Award, worth £5000, is given for an architect's first stand-alone building and is sponsored by *The Architects' Journal* with Robin Ellis Design Build.

It requires courage for an architect to set up on their own after seven years' training plus several in the relatively safe environment of a bigger practice. As well as guts, it needs a lucky break, which ideally means finding a good client. Architects not in that position often choose to produce a little gem of a building as a home, office and showcase for their talents, as did Scampton & Barnett. Four of this year's shortlist were houses, the fifth an insertion into a medieval barn which acts as a visitor centre in a country park.

The Architects' Journal, founded in 1895, is the premier paid-for UK architectural weekly. Robin Ellis Design Build, the award's co-sponsors, are responsible for key parts of the refurbishment of the RIBA's Headquarters in Portland Place, London.

THE 2002 SHORTLIST: Wycoller Visitor Centre, **HAKES ASSOCIATES**; Barnhouse, Highgate, **SUTHERLAND HUSSEY ARCHITECTS**; Fairhazel Gardens, London NW6, **SCAMPTON & BARNETT**; VXO House, Hampstead, **ALISON BROOKS ARCHITECTS**; Brooke Coombes House, London W5, **BURD HAWARD MARSTON ARCHITECTS**.

The winner of the 2002 AJ First Building Award supported by Robin Ellis Design Build is Barnhouse Highgate by Sutherland Hussey Architects

Barnhouse sits behind Highgate High Street in London. This is a house built for its particular clients – Carol and Philip Thomas. Sutherland Hussey Architects have produced a fun design, making the most of some of the clients' preferences, notably for avoiding stairs. A floor sloping down and timber-ramped bridge sloping up create a striking beginning to a house that follows the footprints of the butcher's buildings previously on the site, drawing them together into a group of small, private places and large, open, shared spaces. The house and its pool turn to address distant views, almost Italianate, towards the wooded slopes of exotic Essex, yet its entry is almost hidden on the High Street. More gothic than classic, the colours and textures of largely untreated materials are robust yet tactile. The clients feel thoroughly at home here.

BARNHOUSE PRIVATE RESIDENCE
HIGHGATE

Slip up the alleyways between the buildings on any traditional high street and you'll discover the remnants of the outbuildings that supported the businesses on the front. Behind a butcher's shop in Highgate High Street was a slaughterhouse that, cruelly, gave the beasts their last glimpse of countryside, across the Highgate Bowl. The Barnhouse occupies the same footprint as these original buildings and enjoys the same fine views.

A collaboration between the self-build client and the architects, this is a quirky and personal building. It is conceived as three quite different pavilions, leading one to another and linked by a glazed conservatory opening out on to a small court. The house is reached through a small gateway on the High Street forming an arrival space. Once inside, two ramps begin their journeys through the house, the lower leading to the dining and kitchen areas situated around the linking conservatory and the upper rising to the main living room with its spectacular views from the top of Highgate Hill.

The design retains the somewhat raw quality of the original site and buildings, with each of the linked elements expressed individually through a range of extremely tactile and robustly detailed natural materials. The combination of materials and the variety of interconnecting spaces create a house of rich experience and character, a testament to the understanding that has clearly developed between architect and client.

AJ FIRST BUILDING AWARD

CLIENT private
STRUCTURAL ENGINEER Techniker
CONTRACTOR self-build

CONTRACT VALUE £500,000
PHOTOGRAPHY Philip Thomas

Sutherland Hussey Architects

ADAPT TRUST ACCESS AWARD

The Access Award is sponsored by the ADAPT Trust, and given to the architects of an arts or heritage building that goes beyond the demands of building regulations and provides access for people of all abilities by considering their needs from the outset of a project, not bolting on solutions as an afterthought.

The ADAPT Trust was set up in 1989 following a report by Lord Attenborough on access to arts buildings. It carries out audits on existing buildings and advises on new ones, bearing in mind not just the obvious needs of wheelchair users but those of people with hearing difficulties and visual impairment, whose problems in using buildings can be just as great. It not just a matter of ramps and signs, it is about the whole way spaces relate in buildings, about lateral as well as vertical movement and about the acoustic behaviour of surfaces. It is also about getting value for money by doing the right things at the right time, and not having to resort to costly add-ons.

THE 2002 SHORTLIST: Oldham Art Gallery, **PRINGLE RICHARDS SHARRATT**; Tate Britain Centenary Development, London, **JOHN MILLER & PARTNERS**; Royal Academy of Music, London, **JOHN McASLAN & PARTNERS**; Southwark Cathedral Millennium Project, **RICHARD GRIFFITHS ARCHITECTS**; Stirling Tolbooth, **RICHARD MURPHY ARCHITECTS**; Dance Base, Edinburgh, **MALCOLM FRASER ARCHITECTS**.

The winner of the 2002 ADAPT Trust Access Award is Dance Base, Edinburgh by Malcolm Fraser Architects.

This project presented the architects with a site in 'old town' Edinburgh, not renowned for its accessibility. The result has proved that access issues do not preclude the aesthetics of good design and what impressed the judges most was the way facilities for disabled people have been seamlessly incorporated throughout the building.

In a period when more disabled people want to participate as equals and enjoy the facilities available to everyone else, Dance Base provides this opportunity. Basic physical access has been provided to all levels but it is the design detail that has made this building special. Particular attention has been given to colour effects, signage and hearing-assistive systems, making it a joy for people with sensory impairments to use. The management team has put its accessible building to good use and offers classes for people of all abilities.

All of the projects considered for this year's award show that access issues are now being addressed as an integral part of the overall design. This was the most encouraging aspect for the Trust. The ADAPT Trust also commended the other shortlisted entries, but especially Southwark Cathedral Millennium Project and the Stirling Tolbooth.

For building description see pages 24–26.

THE RIBA JOURNAL
SUSTAINABILITY AWARD

This prize, fully supported by *The RIBA Journal*, is made to the building which demonstrates most elegantly and durably the principles of sustainable architecture. The award is about building for future generations without destroying the world they will grow up in and is given in recognition of the importance of sustainability in architecture today. The prize was established in 2000 when the winners were Chetwood Associates' Sainsbury's at Greenwich. Last year's winner was Michael Hopkins and Partners' Jubilee Campus at the University of Nottingham. This year's panel of expert judges comprised: Amanda Baillieu, Editor of *The RIBA Journal*; Paul Hyett, RIBA President; Ian Davidson, Chair of the RIBA Awards Group; and William Watts of Max Fordham Associates.

The *RIBA Journal* is published monthly by the Builder Group and was recently voted by RIBA members as the most important benefit of membership.

THE 2002 SHORTLIST: Entrance, Planet Earth Galleries and Solar Canopy, The Earth Centre, Doncaster, **FEILDEN CLEGG BRADLEY**; Gateway, Baglan Energy Park, Port Talbot, **NEATH PORT TALBOT CBC**; Cardboard Building, Westcliff-on-Sea, **COTTRELL + VERMEULEN ARCHITECTURE**; Downland Gridshell, Chichester, **EDWARD CULLINAN ARCHITECTS**; Fingal County Offices, Co. Dublin, **BUCHOLZ McEVOY WITH BDP DUBLIN**.

The winner of the 2002 RIBA Journal Sustainability Award is The Cardboard Building, Westborough Primary School, Westcliff-on-Sea by Cottrell + Vermeulen Architecture.

The judges were completely won over by Westborough School's Cardboard building. Europe's first permanent cardboard building, this much-needed educational and community space is also an inspiring structure that works with the properties of the material.

The 750 pupils were involved with the project from the outset, as were a total of 21 different manufacturers and suppliers who either provided materials free of charge, helped with labour and expertise, or subsidised the project. Cardboard tubes are used as structural columns, while the walls and roof are constructed from load bearing and insulating timber-edged cardboard panels. Designed to last for 20 years, the building's layout is inherently flexible, allowing a wide range of uses within the main space.

A school made of cardboard may seem an absurd proposition, but the beauty of it is that it shows the architect's capacity to think laterally, challenging all perceptions about what can or cannot be used as a building material.

Also winner of The Stephen Lawrence Prize. For building description see page 52.

THE RIBA CLIENT OF THE YEAR
SPONSORED BY THE ARTS COUNCIL OF ENGLAND

The RIBA set up the Client of the Year Award five years ago and, apart from the Stirling Prize and the Royal Gold Medal, it is the most important award the Institute makes. Unless the people who commission buildings have vision and faith, there can be no good architecture; everyone has benefitted from the taste and persistence of good clients, from the Medicis to Roland Paoletti.

The Arts Council of England once again supported the award, as it has done from the start. The prize is £5000, to be spent on a contemporary work of art by an artist working in Britain. In this way the prize supports good architects and good artists.

Architecture is a team effort and previous winners have amply demonstrated that: Roland Paoletti, who received the first award for the new Jubilee Line stations; The MCC for commissioning a series of fine buildings at Lord's Cricket Ground; The Foreign and Commonwealth Office for pulling off a series of iconic embassies around the world; and the Molendinar Park Housing Association Glasgow for their campus of buildings by a variety of Scottish architects. All these have proved that producing good buildings is not a one-off trick – they showed they could repeat it.

THE 2002 SHORTLIST: Greater Manchester; Urban Splash; Westborough Primary School; Lady Bessborough, Roche Court; The Tate; Iain Tuckett, Coin Street Community Builders.

The winner of the 2002 RIBA Client of the Year is Urban Splash. The north-west England based development company has an impressive record of seeking out derelict or near-derelict buildings and bringing them back to life through undertaking outstanding regeneration projects. Parts of Manchester and Liverpool have been given new hope as a result of Urban Splash initiatives. Working sometimes with their sister firm of architects, Shed KM and sometimes with other practices such as Stephenson/Bell, they have produced a series of well-designed, RIBA Award-winning projects, including Smithfield Buildings (Manchester, 1998), Old Haymarket (Liverpool, 2001), and Britannia Mills (Manchester, 2001).

For their commitment to both design quality and regeneration, Urban Splash are the 2002 Client of the Year. The firm's RIBA Award-winning buildings this year were the conversions of an old Liverpool school into housing and Matchworks, the old Bryant and May factory, also in Liverpool, into commercial space.

For descriptions of Urban Splash's 2002 RIBA Award-winning buildings see pages 86 and 90.

the riba awards

RIBA AWARDS 2002

RIBA Awards are given for excellence rather than size or complexity. Jurors are encouraged to include buildings that are otherwise unlikely to come to public notice. Awards are judged regionally by a series of panels consisting of an architect of national renown (not from that region), a local architect, and a non-architect (the lay juror).

Fifty-eight RIBA Award winners in the UK and elsewhere in the European Union were announced in June 2002 at an Awards Dinner held at the International Convention Centre in Birmingham, during the RIBA's Conference. The following section illustrates and describes, geographically from north to south, all of those 58 winners which did not also win additional prizes or were not shortlisted for the RIBA Stirling Prize. These are shown elsewhere in this book.

Each winner is presented with certificates for the client, key consultants and contractor at ceremonies throughout the 14 RIBA regions. They also receive a lead plaque to affix to the building. These have been produced by The Lead Sheet Association for 12 years and the RIBA is grateful for the Association's continuing support.

BASEMENT FLAT, MORAY PLACE
EDINBURGH

Only in Edinburgh would an inner-city basement flat enjoy spectacular views across a wooded valley to winding neo-classical terraces, all framed on one side by mountains.

This wonderful conversion and extension of a New Town basement flat exploits the position and topography of its site to the full to create a single new domestic interior with kitchen, dining area and living room, each occupying a discrete level stepping down to the garden. The detailing of the interior is restrained but endlessly inventive, providing places to display objects, keep books and show drawings, paintings and collections of glasses. The entire space is flooded with natural light from a series of rooflights carefully inserted into or alongside the lead-covered vaulted roof that encloses the interior. And in a typically thoughtful and imaginative way, each of these rooflights can be blacked out with a plywood shutter, operated by satisfyingly mechanical winding gear embedded in the walls, to change the atmosphere of the interior in the evening. Great glass doors slide into the walls to open up the flat to the terrace on warm days, blurring the inside–outside transition in a masterly way.

To live here is obviously a complete delight: this is a building that works well in every detail. The clients, a former Secretary of the RIBA and his wife, are delighted with the way the scheme enhances their daily life. This was one of those projects, they say, which grew and grew, but they have no regrets: the experience has been life-changing and shows how good architecture always gives the client a little more than they knew they wanted. Shortlisted for The Stephen Lawrence Prize.

SCOTLAND

CLIENTS Patrick and Mary Harrison
STRUCTURAL ENGINEER David Narro Associates
QS Morham & Brotchie

CONTRACTOR Inscape Joinery
CONTRACT VALUE £178,000
PHOTOGRAPHY David Churchill

Richard Murphy Architects

BYRE THEATRE
ST ANDREWS

The Byre theatre began life as a cow-shed. In 1933 the stone building on the edge of St Andrews town centre was converted into a theatre and by 1989 it had an auditorium seating 174. Front- and back-of-house facilities were equally poor and the advent of the Lottery brought the chance to create the 'best small theatre in Scotland.' That at least was what the 1995 competition brief specified. It also called for the intimate atmosphere to be retained, with a modest increase in capacity to 220 seats, while radically improving all the other facilities, and for the theatre to be made fully accessible. Another challenge came from the site, which straddles two roads, a busy thoroughfare, and a pedestrian way.

The architects responded by creating an internal street linking the two, with a new public entrance on the busy Abbey Street, where the new building is on a modest, domestic scale, and rear access to a secret garden on South Court. The performance space, with enlarged stage and full fly tower, is enclosed within an in-situ concrete drum. Around the theatre are arranged a series of foyer spaces with bars and cafés, as well as efficient new backstage areas, offices and rehearsal space. The theatre and the foyers make a wonderful contrast: the former enclosed, dark and intimate; the latter open, generous and day-lit by a succession of carefully placed rooflights and windows. The result is an excellent new theatre and a busy public forum, all created without losing the sense of intimacy and intensity that were so much a part of the original theatre.

SCOTLAND

STRUCTURAL ENGINEER Babtie Group
M&E ENGINEER Babtie Group
QS DI Burchell & Partners
LIGHTING DPA Lighting
ACOUSTICS New Acoustics

THEATRE CONSULTANT DPA Technical Services
CONTRACTOR Laing Ltd
CONTRACT VALUE £4 million
PHOTOGRAPHY Keith Hunter Photography

Nicoll Russell Studios

CENTRE FOR CONTEMPORARY ARTS, SAUCIEHALL STREET
GLASGOW

This project took the core of the existing accommodation of the Centre for Contemporary Art in a 'Greek' Thompson building on Glasgow's busy Sauciehall Street and extended it to the rear, incorporating a number of other buildings and the spaces between them. In this way the architects have subtly created additional and improved facilities, as well as new connections and entrances which encourage greater accessibility and use.

Most dramatically the scheme opened up a single-storey courtyard space in the centre of the plan to create a roof-lit atrium. This forms the new heart of the centre, around which all of the facilities of the arts centre are located. Here, the complex architectural history of the site is dramatically exposed as the façades of buildings previously hidden can contribute to the framing and enclosure of this wonderful new space, which now includes a restaurant. Because the cross-streets climb like those of San Francisco, the 'building within a building' is propped up, its front door opening on to a gallery at first-floor level in the atrium. Further up the hill, a self-contained bar fronts on to the side street.

The architecture of the new work is restrained where the activities it houses or the presence of existing buildings require it, but is powerful and provocative when appropriate opportunities arise. Most impressive of all is the consistency of the architectural language: this is a building that is both very carefully thought through and excellently built. Shortlisted for the Crown Estate Conservation Award.

STRUCTURAL ENGINEER Arup Scotland
M&E ENGINEER Harley Haddow
QS RM Neilson Partnership
LIGHTING CONSULTANT Kevan Shaw Lighting Design

ACOUSTIC DESIGN Arup Acoustics
CONTRACTOR Lilley Construction
CONTRACT VALUE £6 million
PHOTOGRAPHY Keith Hunter Photography

Page and Park Architects

MOUNT STUART VISITORS' CENTRE
ISLE OF BUTE

The client, 1987 Le Mans winner Johnny Bute, wanted a building to excite as well as accommodate visitors to his family seat, Mount Stuart House. The architects proposed a wall that could be walked on, providing vantage points from which to view the big house and the Clyde. It was completed within a year.

Placed at right angles to the route, the visitor centre contains within its timber-clad base a reception area, auditorium, exhibition space, toilets, and a shop. From here, a stair leads to the restaurant on the first floor, a glass pavilion enclosed by an extraordinary cantilevered steel roof. The restaurant terrace exploits the fall in the land to connect this upper level directly to the hillside, where a children's playground has been placed.

Externally, the building is meticulously detailed, combining restraint in the articulation of the surfaces with seductive selection of form and materials. On a spring morning it is both welcoming and calm; at night it scintillates in the landscape. The interior is, in many ways, very simple, but is obviously very considered. Everything is carefully planned and clearly works exceptionally well. Again, materials are sensitively chosen; even the exposed steel decking which forms the underside of the concrete floor slab contributes to the interior's confident clarity. The lightweight roof was devised by Anthony Hunt; its hull-like strength depends on an egg-crate form of quarter-inch ply applied in three layers.

This is a building for everybody and is clearly already much enjoyed and loved by those who commissioned it.

CLIENT Mount Stuart Trust Ltd
STRUCTURAL ENGINEER Anthony Hunt Associates
SERVICES ENGINEER Atelier Ten

QS Doig & Smith
CONTRACTOR Thomas Johnstone Ltd
CONTRACT VALUE £1 million
PHOTOGRAPHY Keith Hunter Photography

Munkenbeck + Marshall

SCIENCE CENTRE, PACIFIC QUAY
GLASGOW

Like the Stirling Prize-winning Magna in Rotherham, BDP's Science Centre is inspired by the four elements: earth, expressed in the science mall; water in the IMAX theatre; air in the revolving GSC tower; and fire in the imagination that informs the whole project.

The Science Centre is one of a series of projects destined to bring new life to the banks of the Clyde. What is most spectacular about the buildings is their form: steel lattice shell structures clad in titanium, lying like pebbles in the developing landscape. They are potent symbols of both regeneration and the buildings' technological content. Inside a vivid, stimulating environment encourages exploration of the various exhibitions and displays. And one of the best displays is the city itself, revealed by a huge expanse of glazing which cuts in a single plane across the northern face of the main building.

The tower, built according to Richard Horden's competition-winning concept, rotates through 360 degrees according to wind direction. An observation cabin 120 metres above the Clyde provides for still more remarkable views. The IMAX appears to float in a water garden and is perched precariously over the basin. It is linked to the science mall by a glazed entrance box with a wave-like stretched fabric roof. A discovery tunnel connects the mall and tower. The buildings are intended as exhibits in their own right and aim to complement the ethos of the project, which is to demystify science through hands-on, interactive experience. This is truly a machine for learning in.

CLIENT Glasgow Science Centre Ltd
STRUCTURAL ENGINEERS WA Fairhurst & Partners/Buro Happold
M&E ENGINEERS Cundall Johnston & Partners/Buro Happold
LIGHTING Jonathan Speirs Associates

QS Doig & Smith/Davis Langdon & Everest
CONTRACTOR Carillion Building
CONTRACT VALUE £38 million
PHOTOGRAPHY Keith Hunter Photography

SCOTLAND

Building Design Partnership

GREAT HALL RESTORATION, QUEEN'S UNIVERSITY
BELFAST

A century and a half after the Irish architect Lanyon designed the Great Hall for the new Queen's University, his work has finally been finished. The University ran out of money and much of the detailing, including the panelling, remained unfinished.

It is hard not to be impressed by the grandeur and elegance of what Consarc have done to complete and restore this great dining hall. The interior was drab, despite the half-height panelling painted pink. It has been completely rethought, with an increase in the height of the enclosing dado panelling, flooring, lighting and colouring of the whole. This is no slavish restoration; it is far truer to the spirit of the original architect's intentions than what was there before. Modern chandeliers illumine the fine hammer-beam trusses one of which was replaced – precisely which it is impossible to tell. Portraits of the university's great and good line the walls, using a hanging system incorporated into the panelling. A new lift gives access down to the kitchens in the extended basement, to the gallery soon to house an organ by Lanyon rescued from a disused church, and a newly created long gallery to house paintings from the university's collections.

The restoration has proved very popular with both students and staff and uniquely is open to the public for lunches and is already a popular venue. The funding for this particular project was entirely raised privately, a remarkable tribute to the local importance of this fine building.

Shortlisted for the Crown Estate Conservation Award.

NORTHERN IRELAND

STRUCTURAL ENGINEER Peter Fitzpatrick
M&E ENGINEER AH Design
QS Hood Magowan Kirk
CONTRACTOR Felix O'Hare Ltd

CONTRACT VALUE £1.5 million
PHOTOGRAPHY Ivan Ewart, Q U B Media Services

Consarc Conservation

RESIDENTIAL DEVELOPMENT, SANDY ROW
BELFAST

Sandy Row is linked to the Unionist tradition and the architects of this multi-use private development have deliberately placed the main entrance on the traditionally neutral Malone Place. The result is an unexpected contribution to the fabric of the city, combining regeneration of street life with the creation of a calm inner courtyard, around which the accommodation is arranged. Each of the four façades is conceived within a simple red-brick palette of materials and scale, which relate neatly to the adjacent context of apartment, warehouse, two-storey houses and terraces. It is impressive how this modest menu is adapted to meet the street, particularly at a difficult junction of the plinth car park next to the warehousing.

The true quality of this scheme lies in the elevated courtyard accessed by lift and stair foyers. The contrast could not be greater: residents are raised from the frenetic street activity into a new special space. White-rendered façades of various rhythms and proportions address a tapering rectangular space of pebbles, planted boxes and pool. This reflective space, edged on two sides by three-storey interlinking pavilions and two-storey canted-back roof penthouses, frames the higher-level accommodation at the tapered end and the lower block to the south. Crucially, this lets more sunlight into the courtyard and confirms the drop in scale to the terrace in Malone Place.

This development would grace any city and could serve as a model for further regeneration in Belfast and beyond.

CLIENT Carvill Group Ltd
STRUCTURAL ENGINEER Fergus Gilligan & Partners
M&E ENGINEER Beattie Flanigan & Partners

LANDSCAPE Nicholas Pearson Associates
CONTRACTOR Carvill Group
CONTRACT VALUE £7.5 million
PHOTOGRAPHY Todd Watson, Signals Design & Photography

Todd Architects

COLLEGIATE REGENERATION
LIVERPOOL

Harvey Lonsdale Elmes designed the Collegiate School in 1843 in the then fashionable neo-gothic style. After it closed in 1986, the building suffered extensive fire damage. By the time Urban Splash bought it, the grade II*-listed structure was a blackened shell. The architects had to come up with a solution that would save the old school from demolition.

Their answer was to keep the massive sandstone walls and to construct a new free-standing apartment building behind. The glass skin is glimpsed through the retained tracery of the unglazed windows. Other elements of the building's history, a scholarship board and a fireplace, have also been saved and strategically placed in the foyer and on the first-floor landing and the remains of the separate octagonal theatre have been turned into a first floor garden. Its zen-like calm is due not only to the restrained planting but also to lack of use, at least on the days the judges visited. It is hard to imagine this haunted, empty space thronged with sunbathing yuppies, but the building as a whole would make a good home to some latter-day Goths, who might relish its melancholy feel.

The one- and two-bed apartments are cleverly designed around double-height spaces. The architects have mastered the knack of using inexpensive finishes to convey a sense of space and luxury, in what are relatively small units. In some ways, this is the best bit of the design and the judges thought the new build might well have deserved an award even without its ruined cousin.

Urban Splash is RIBA Client of the Year.

CLIENT Urban Splash
STRUCTURAL ENGINEERS Curtin Consulting Engineers/Buro Happold
M&E ENGINEER Steven Hunt & Associates
QS Simon Fenton Partnership

CONTRACTORS Totty Construction Group/Maysand
CONTRACT £9 million
PHOTOGRAPHY Nick Hufton Photography/VIEW

Shed KM

MANCHESTER INTERNATIONAL CONVENTION CENTRE

The International Convention Centre was planned as a complement to the huge GMEX Centre in the old station next door but it works as a stand-alone facility as well as an extension to its neighbour. It was made possible by funding from the City Council, English Partnerships and the European Regional Development Fund. The team of two practices was appointed in 1997; local firm Stephenson Bell designed the envelope and the landscaping and London practice Sheppard Robson were responsible for the internal design. Construction began in January 1999 and the first delegates were welcomed in April 2001.

The architecture expresses the clear geometry of the two main elements of an 800-seat auditorium and 1800 square metres of exhibition space. The secondary elements, along with the circulation, are used to accommodate the awkward shape of the site. The joining of these shapes is exploited by the architects to generate a series of architectural compositions, with the building knitting together disparate parts of the site. A lovely delicate canopy celebrates the drama of arrival. Mass and transparency are handled with skill and there is coherence to the area around the building.

An enlightened client, the City of Manchester is well aware that effective regeneration requires good architecture and the completed scheme is an unequivocal piece of modern architecture in a Victorian context. The centre has already been one of the key venues for the 2002 Commonwealth Games, housing the weightlifting and, still more onerously perhaps, the press centre.

Greater Manchester Council, shortlisted for RIBA Client of the Year.

NORTH-WEST

CLIENT Manchester City Council
STRUCTURAL ENGINEER Arup
M&E ENGINEER Arup
QS Davis Langdon & Everest

CONTRACTOR Carillion Building
CONTRACT VALUE £23 million
PHOTOGRAPHY Peter Cook/VIEW

Stephenson Bell/Sheppard Robson

MATCHWORKS, SPEKE ROAD
LIVERPOOL

The project involved conversion of the partially listed Bryant and May match factory into office space. The main building was engineered by Sven Bylander and is an early example of flat-slab concrete construction. The original building had glorious spaces dominated by a regular grid of high concrete columns. The brief was to insert mezzanine floors to maximise lettable accommodation and to introduce regular services for subdivision into individual office units. In less able hands, this could have proved an act of vandalism.

A steel beam, elegantly fixed to the old columns, supports the new mezzanine floors. The toilets, kitchens and stairs are expressed as a bold series of cylindrical volumes projecting from the rear. During judging, the floor spaces were altogether clear, awaiting the arrival of the call centres, with their inevitable detrimental visual impact.

In a way, very little has been done. Everything that has been done has been executed with a clear vigour. The architects have developed a language of primary forms based on the cylinder. Benches, reception desks, balustrades and service cores are expressed as a family of tough objects. The point is that the clear architectural intention will remain legible, even when the building is overwhelmed by soft furnishings and contract interiors.

This building shows that it is possible to operate with wit and clarity, even within very narrow margins. It is a wonderfully sturdy old building, given robust treatment by its new architects.

Urban Splash is RIBA Client of the Year.

NORTH-WEST

CLIENT Urban Splash
STRUCTURAL ENGINEER Roy Billingtons Associates
QS Simon Fenton Partnership
LANDSCAPE ARCHITECT McAllister

CONTRACTOR Urban Splash Projects
CONTRACT VALUE £5.5 million
PHOTOGRAPHY Nick Hulton Photography/VIEW

Shed KM

OLDHAM ART GALLERY

The Gallery is part of a proposed four-phase development intended to establish a new 'cultural quarter' in Oldham. The three-storey structure links in with an existing collection of public buildings to form a new square. The architects related the scale and form of the new building to older mill buildings, now demolished, visible in a nineteenth-century panoramic photograph of the site displayed in the bridge between old and new buildings.

The new building contains galleries, education and administration rooms, art stores, and a café. The galleries are on the top floor, bypassing two lower floors of ancillary accommodation and linking into a library building next door. You enter from a small landscaped square, into a high glazed atrium and take generous lifts up to the galleries with a lovely view over the town. The spacious top-lit galleries run the length of the building and are the main pleasure of the project. They are flanked by an array of metal hoops enclosing external walkways providing views of the town and the Pennines; sadly these are only accessible with special permission. The plain solidity of the detailing lends a reassuring and substantial civic quality. Accessibility is good throughout.

The jury enjoyed the quiet dignity of the galleries. They were impressed by the client's enthusiasm for her architects. They thought that the new square, invented out of nothing by the architects, was a delight on a cool, sunny April morning. This building, popular with the locals, is a well-made and brings some coherence to a difficult site. Shortlisted for the ADAPT Trust Access Award.

CLIENT Oldham Art Gallery
STRUCTURAL ENGINEER Arup
M&E ENGINEER Arup
QS Davis Langdon & Everest
ACCESS CONSULTANT Buro Happold

LANDSCAPING Camlin Lonsdale/OMBC
CONTRACTOR Mowlem Management
CONTRACT VALUE £8 million
PHOTOGRAPHY Edmund Sumner Photography

Pringle Richards Sharratt Ltd

WYCOLLER VISITORS' CENTRE

LANCASHIRE

Wycoller Hall was a favourite destination of the Brontës on their long walks and Charlotte used it as the model for Fearndean Manor in *Jane Eyre*. Like many good workaday buildings, the stone barn has seen a number of changes of use. The huge openings in the oak-framed structure helped the threshing process; in the nineteenth century they admitted the gentry's carriages. Today they are glazed – by simply pinning clear glass to the outside of the building – and let light into a visitor centre for the country park.

The RIBA held an open competition for the conversion of this seventeenth-century barn. Lancashire County Council wished to install heated accommodation for an attendant, performance space, information display and provide disabled access. Hakes Associates, a small local practice with no track record of completed buildings, was appointed.

The barn is a medieval timber-aisled structure on stone walls with a cobbled floor. The insertions sit like good pieces of modern furniture in an old room without destroying the spirit of the place, examples of architectural tact and invention. Discrete, prefabricated components – display case, ramp, stage, shelter – are inserted into the barn as free-standing elements. The repair and restoration work was carried out by local craftsmen using local stone, sheep's wool (for insulation) and timber that was reclaimed or came from Forest Stewardship Council-approved sources, materials which should age well with the building. Client and jury agreed that the spirit of the old barn remained intact. Shortlisted for the AJ First Building Award and The Stephen Lawrence Prize.

CLIENT Lancashire County Council
STRUCTURAL ENGINEER Whitby Bird & Partners
ARCHAEOLOGICAL CONSULTANT David Michaelmore

ECOLOGICAL CONSULTANT Stan Irwin
CONTRACTOR Pro-Craft Ltd
CONTRACT VALUE £105,000
PHOTOGRAPHY Max Alexander

NORTH-WEST

Hakes Associates

ENTRANCE, PLANET EARTH GALLERIES AND SOLAR CANOPY
THE EARTH CENTRE, DONCASTER

The 120-hectare site is one of the most environmentally and socially devastated in the country, part of the once-proud South Yorkshire coalfield. The Earth Centre aims to provide information about the environment in an entertaining way; its architecture – including a café, shop, public facilities, an information point and exhibition spaces – aims to demonstrate the principles of low-energy environmental design. It is clear that the architects have got into the spirit of the place. Here 'sustainability meets aesthetics' demonstrates that sustainability can provide all the elements of good architecture.

The entrance building is a simple but beautifully detailed box, finished in a combination of glazing and 'green oak' slats. The gallery is trapezoidal in plan and is enveloped in local limestone, mimicking the nearby escarpment where the stone was quarried. Between the two buildings, a photovoltaic canopy sits upon a complex and exciting timber structure, whose shadows create an abstract representation of a living forest.

In terms of sustainability, the building is packed with innovative ideas: the raft foundations developed into a basement labyrinth as a heat store in winter and cooler in summer; the canopy with four types of embedded photovoltaic cells providing an enormous amount of electric power; the buildings buried underground; minimum water wastage with on-site reedbed water treatment; and limestone quarried 500 metres away.

In its response to the brief, its execution and its interaction with its setting, the building scores highly.

Shortlisted for The RIBA Journal Sustainability Award.

YORKSHIRE

STRUCTURAL ENGINEER Atelier One
M&E ENGINEER Atelier Ten
QS Bernard Williams Associates
LANDSCAPE ARCHITECT Grant Associates

CONTRACTOR Bovis Construction
(arrivals); Taylor Woodrow (canopy)
CONTRACT VALUE £8 million
PHOTOGRAPHY Dennis Gilbert

Feilden Clegg Bradley Architects LLP

PERSISTENCE WORKS
SHEFFIELD

The UK's first purpose-built fine art and craft studio complex, Persistence Works is the brainchild of the client Kate Dore. This bold new infill building is located at the junction of cultural and industrial developments within the old cutlery quarter of the city. The architects describe it as a 'synthesis of the two aspects of the cultural and industrial quarter.'

The brief called for a low-energy, low-maintenance facility which would provide sufficient lettable studio space to obviate the need for revenue funding. It is constructed from cast in-situ concrete, and is based on two parallel blocks either side of an internal street – one of two storeys, the other of six – reflecting the surrounding industrial buildings. The form and its adventurous use of concrete – its first use by the practice – is a clear expression of its function, as well as being appropriate symbolically.

Much of the architectural metalwork was carried out by, or in collaboration with, the occupying artists. The building sits well in the streetscape and is something of a landmark in the area. The glazed screen to the front elevation is particularly dramatic at night.

The jury was impressed by the legibility of the plan and the three-dimensional characteristics of the internal spaces. The relationship of internal and external spaces, the way daylight penetrated and the logical arrangement of accommodation all made for good architecture. The street was skilfully handled and the whole of the interior well thought out and robustly detailed, with thematic consistency.

YORKSHIRE

CLIENT Yorkshire Artspace Society
STRUCTURAL ENGINEER Buro Happold
M&E ENGINEER Buro Happold
QS Citex
LANDSCAPE ARCHITECT Grant Associates

ACCESS CONSULTANT All Clear Designs Ltd
CONTRACTOR M J Gleeson
CONTRACT VALUE £4.25 million
PHOTOGRAPHY Stuart Blackwood

Feilden Clegg Bradley Architects LLP

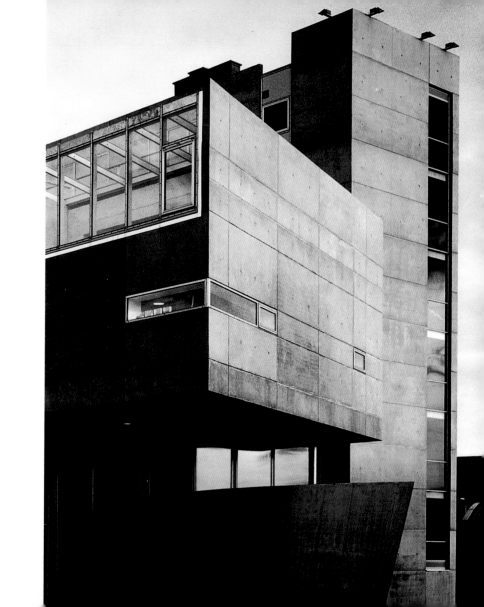

GATEWAY DEVELOPMENT, BAGLAN ENERGY PARK
PORT TALBOT

Making high-quality architecture at around £600 per square metre is quite an achievement. When the building is also an exemplar of sustainable environmental design, it is surely worth an award. The gateway building to the Baglan Energy Park was designed to demonstrate energy efficiency and set design standards for a regeneration project that will transform the area, once a BP chemical factory. The building is robust and simple – even repetitive – with extensions housing staircases and fire escapes as well as providing natural light and ventilation openings. The jury was impressed by the logical simplicity of the environmental strategy in the south-facing offices. Windows shaded by photovoltaic awnings are manually operated combining with cross-ventilating north wall 'chimneys'. An automatic version of the same type of system is used throughout the production area.

Daylighting was modelled in detail with the help of an artificial sky at Cardiff University, and the building was calculated to have a 2.1 per cent daylight factor. Both the daylighting and the ventilation system provided what appeared to be a healthy working environment. The cladding changes colour with the weather, providing visual interest by day. The façade incorporates 100 square metres of photovoltaic panels, a useful demonstration of an emerging technology. They also help to justify the use of a spectacular external lighting system that at night becomes a fluorescent blue, ensuring the visual success of the landmark at night as well as day.

Shortlisted for The RIBA Journal Sustainability Award.

CLIENT Neath Port Talbot CBC
ENVIRONMENTAL DESIGN Professor Phil Jones and Dr Wayne Forster, Cardiff University, Centre for Research in the Built Environment

CONTRACTOR Interserve Building (formerly Tilbury Douglas Construction)
CONTRACT VALUE £2.4 million
PHOTOGRAPHY Peter S Jones, Gower Photographic Studios

Director of Technical Services, Neath Port Talbot CBC

BIRMINGHAM HIPPODROME THEATRE REDEVELOPMENT

This project is an object lesson in creating order from chaos. Taking up virtually the whole of a city block, the Hippodrome consisted of a ramshackle series of sites of varying size: the existing 1800-seat auditorium, ancillary space and the 1980s home of the Birmingham Royal Ballet. The architect has skilfully knitted these elements into a cohesive whole that clearly delights the client, met his brief admirably and provided good value for money at a cost of £1850 per square metre.

The scheme retains the auditorium and arranges the new accommodation, including a 206-seat studio theatre and two dance studios, around a six-storey atrium, bringing light to all floors including the basement. Even the dressing rooms, usually depressing and windowless, have views over an internal garden.

The main elevation clearly signals the theatrical nature of the building and makes a positive contribution to an extremely low-grade urban context. A clear progression of distinct yet open spaces lead from the entrance through the foyers to the auditoria. The central four-storey atrium space is particularly successful, incorporating a glazed clerestorey and a fritted glazed wall-cum-artwork by Liz Rideal. The other atrium provides light and focus for all the back-of-house facilities in a much plainer, yet no less successful, way. Colour is used to create clear routes through this highly complex and labyrinthine building. Improved accessibility escape routes have also been skilfully incorporated.

WEST MIDLANDS

CLIENT Birmingham Hippodrome Theatre Trust
STRUCTURAL ENGINEER Buro Happold
M&E ENGINEER Buro Happold
QS EC Harris
ACOUSTICS Sandy Brown Associates

ACCESS CONSULTANT Earnscliffe Davies Associates
CONTRACTOR HBG Construction (Midlands)
CONTRACT VALUE £18 million
PHOTOGRAPHY Martine Hamilton-Knight

Associated Architects/LDN Architects

SECRET HILLS DISCOVERY CENTRE
CRAVEN ARMS, SHROPSHIRE

Visitor centres have become a building type in themselves in these days of lottery funding; by no means are they all as good as this one, developed out of the Shropshire Rural Tourism Project. It sits quietly yet confidently in its surroundings, fulfilling its purpose, 'to tell the story of the Shropshire hills', without being visually aggressive. It wears its environmental credentials – another part of the educative process – very much on its sleeve.

The pair of curved grass roofs makes reference to the many hill forts found in the region. Striking close-up, they virtually disappear at a distance. The exhibition cone (home to a balloon ride) pokes 8 metres above the roofs and is vertically clad in timber. The curved glazed circulation spine is a particularly successful element, its orientation ensuring a play of light and shadow on the adjacent wall on sunny days. Its round form avoids the front–back problem that so many public buildings suffer from: here there is no back to disappoint. The relatively spare palette of materials is detailed in a workman-like way, in keeping with the ethos of building and client. The progression of spaces through the relatively dark reception area to the bright, light café space draws the visitor in.

The building forms a gateway to The Meadows, a landscape project which encourages engagement with the natural world, but the centre has become a destination in its own right, providing a lively community focus, a wonderful accolade for any building.

WEST MIDLANDS

CLIENT Shropshire County Council
STRUCTURAL ENGINEER Whitby Bird & Partners
M&E ENGINEER Whitby Bird & Partners
QS Gardiner & Theobald

LANDSCAPE ARCHITECT Eden Design
CONTRACTOR Frank Galliers Ltd
CONTRACT VALUE £1.4 million
PHOTOGRAPHY David Lewis

Niall Phillips Architects

NEW GIRLS' BOARDING HOUSES
HAILEYBURY AND IMPERIAL SERVICE COLLEGE

The college took the decision to go co-educational in 1997, and had to find a way to accommodate up to 120 girls within two years. This was also to be a flagship project, one that demanded a sensitive design response, with a realistic budget and a favoured site in parkland designed by Repton. The result is a success on many levels. The buildings sit in a natural hollow in mature woodland beside a small pond as if they had always been there. This is a scheme that truly embraces its natural setting.

Architecture is key to all well-run communities but especially to boarding schools, with their potential for conflict and loneliness, as well as friendship. A boarding house must have its own identity, like a family home. The two-storey brick façade with its simple punched windows has been treated with discipline, standing clear of the sloping ground, allowing the garden level to emerge before cantilevering boldly over the pond. The buildings are positioned so that the trees brush against the façades. Fully glazed common rooms at the end of each block exploit the views and are linked by carefully detailed external steel stairs to the pond-level decks. A single-storey sweep of timber-clad grass-roofed community spaces links both wings and encloses the private lawn.

The scale, materials and sympathetic use of the site admirably meet its objectives. While the site is superb, the spatial handling, massing and generally consistent detailing match it. The whole thing has been done with confidence, maturity and panache.

STRUCTURAL ENGINEER Dewhurst Macfarlane & Partners

M&E ENGINEER Max Fordham LLP

LANDSCAPE ARCHITECT FIRA Landscape Architecture and Urban Design

QS Spicer Partnership

CONTRACTOR Willmott Dixon Construction

CONTRACT VALUE £5.9 million

PHOTOGRAPHY Peter Cook/VIEW

Studio E Architects Ltd

QUAKER BARNS, HAVERINGLAND
NORWICH

The barn conversion is a much-derided building type – not least by planners. This conversion of disused agricultural buildings into two holiday homes will not only persuade planners to grant more such permissions but will contribute to the local economy.

The architects have cleverly avoided the common fault in such conversions of domesticating the buildings too much; here their agricultural history is still plain. It was the consistency of the execution of the conversion that impressed the jury. The concept, setting and detail demonstrate thoughtfulness, restraint and wit.

The buildings sit comfortably next to their listed neighbours. The simplicity of the landscaping blends the buildings with the rolling countryside, the boundary marked by an elegant agricultural metal fence. A surprising amount of accommodation is effortlessly provided in a series of well-proportioned spaces. The existing building fabric has been carefully repaired using local materials, most of it (and the contractors) coming from within a five-mile radius of the property. The resulting reduction in embodied energy costs is matched by a reduction in running costs through good insulation and the use of solar gain through orientation.

All new construction is minimal in its detail, inventive and waiting to be discovered by the users. Traditional brick ventilation details bring filtered light and privacy to a bathroom. Straw bales, protected by elegantly framed fibreglass sheets, show off the construction. The floor is a stone chip set in resin, almost a frozen version of the original. This is a building that cannot fail to bring enjoyment to its users.
Shortlisted for The Stephen Lawrence Prize.

CLIENT Jenny Hudson
STRUCTURAL ENGINEER Alcock Lees Partnership

CONTRACTOR direct labour
CONTRACT VALUE £190,000
PHOTOGRAPHY Mark Luscombe-Whyte

Hudson Featherstone

THE WILLIAM GATES BUILDING, UNIVERSITY OF CAMBRIDGE

A building should not only be fit for purpose, it should look as if it is. The activities of the university's computer faculty are clearly demonstrated through the creation of this carefully organised complex conceived with simplicity and underplayed grandeur.

Wings of research facilities form two quadrangles of different sizes, with simple hard landscaping and formal planting creating calm contemplative spaces. Thick, heavily insulated walls allow the building to be heated by the occupants. At the end of each brick-clad wing, researchers can relax or work in casual spaces opening up on to well-detailed outside terraces. The security of these facilities is emphasised by the bridge access from the central 'street', which also connects the lecture theatres, teaching spaces and restaurant. These uses are confidently expressed on the public face of the building.

Terracotta-clad seminar rooms have panels peeled away to provide diffused light to the computer users. Lecture theatres clad in timber provide a decked terrace to the fully glazed first-floor teaching space. The timber roof structure of the three-storey building oversails this group on elegantly slim columns and provides solar shading to the glazed south and west.

The overall concept and massing, spatial organisation and refined details – internal and external – produce a well considered whole. The brief called for a building sensitive to energy use and sustainability, and it has achieved this.

EAST

STRUCTURAL ENGINEER RMJM
M&E ENGINEER RMJM
QS Gardiner and Theobald

CONTRACTOR Shepherd Construction Ltd
CONTRACT VALUE £15 million
PHOTOGRAPHY Peter Cook/VIEW

RMJM

LYNHER DAIRY
TRURO

This is an unusual commission for so young a practice and the clients should be congratulated on taking a punt on almost unknown architects from the other end of the UK. The brief called for a highly flexible building that would provide a pleasant working environment and meet the exacting standards of hygiene required by supermarket customers.

One of the company's main products is Cornish yarg, a local nettle-wrapped hard cheese. Cheese-making is a linear process: milk arrives at one end of the building and cheese is dispatched at the other. The building's linear form directly translates the function in an elegant and restrained way. A predominantly single-storey pitched-roof structure, it reflects the scale of the surrounding farm buildings.

For reasons of sustainability, the manufacturers wanted production to be entirely local and so called for the conversion of existing buildings too. A two-storey mono-pitched service core intersects the production building at right angles and distributes services through the pitched roof void. The building makes an elegant point of using industrial components; a highly functional galvanised steel frame is clad with timber boarding and fibrous cement panels.

The building displays an honesty and integrity with regard to its form and expression. It sits well on the site and allows easy expansion. The building's programme coincided with the foot and mouth outbreak which makes its success still more noteworthy. Lynher Dairy is an excellent contemporary interpretation of the industrial vernacular: elegant, fit for its purpose and a delightful response to the brief.

SOUTH-WEST

CLIENT Catherine Mead
STRUCTURAL ENGINEER John Knevitt Practice Ltd

CONTRACTOR Chris Hodgeson Engineering
CONTRACT VALUE £350,000
PHOTOGRAPHY Morley Von Sternberg

Sutherland Hussey Architects

ARTISTS' HOUSE, ROCHE COURT
SALISBURY

The New Art Gallery at Roche Court is a commercial gallery, designed by Munkenbeck + Marshall. It won the Stephen Lawrence Prize in 1999. The new brief called for an infill building providing overnight accommodation for visiting artists and a domestic setting for the display and sale of post-war contemporary art and sculpture. It forms a marked contrast with the larger, public spaces of the sculpture gallery, with its huge folding doors.

The new two-storey building replaces a series of disparate outbuildings and involved the excavation of an earth bank to the rear. But the more challenging part of the brief called for a clearer route around the walled gardens and open lawns. The artists' house acts as a marker, by filling a gap and opening out in one direction on to a courtyard shaded by a giant magnolia tree and in the other to the sloping lawn. Visitors now have a clear circulation route through the existing sculpture garden.

The form and scale complement extremely well the context of the existing house and gardens. The choice of building materials reflects those used within the old house: render, natural stone and oak. The details are well composed and display workmanship, integrity and clarity. The connection between internal and external space and the visual flow between the two environments are the key generators for the building. The resolution is extremely well handled.

The building has a serenity and beauty matched only by the original house and gardens; it is everything it should be. The client has added another fine building to the collection which has surprised and delighted large numbers of visitors already.
Lady Bessborough was shortlisted for the RIBA Client of the Year Award.

WESSEX

CLIENT Lady Bessborough
ENGINEER Harvey & Snowdon
CONTRACTOR Martin Price Period

Renovation and Construction
CONTRACT VALUE £240,000
PHOTOGRAPHY Richard Bryant/ARCAID

Munkenbeck + Marshall

THE POINT, WAPPING WHARF
BRISTOL

The Point is a residential development, comprising 105 one- and two-bedroom apartments, together with nine linked four-storey town houses and a café. The site on the north side of the floating harbour is an important but sadly long under-exploited one.

The development is articulated as three primary forms: a linear block of apartments sits perpendicular to the wharf and screens the site from an existing car park; a triangular block sits by the harbour and points towards the city centre; and a further linear strip of town houses and apartments is placed parallel to, but set back from the water's edge. The composition sits comfortably within its context and creates a series of new hard landscaped spaces between the buildings and the water. Equally importantly, the public is welcomed in through clear gaps between the buildings, their route defined by espaliered trees, which also afford privacy for the householders.

The apartments are generous spatially, with a high level of fit-out. The design of the town houses utilises double-height spaces and roof terraces to maximise solar gain and take full advantage of the magnificent views of the city this scheme enhances. This is a scheme which allows Bristolians to recapture an important part of their public realm.

WESSEX

CLIENT Crosby Homes (Special Projects) Ltd
STRUCTURAL ENGINEER Clarke Bond Partnership
LANDSCAPE ARCHITECT Cooper Partnership Ltd

M&E ENGINEER BME Partnership
CONTRACTOR Skanska Construction Group Ltd
CONTRACT VALUE £14.5 million
PHOTOGRAPHY Peter Cook/VIEW

Feilden Clegg Bradley Architects LLP

ARTIGIANO DESIGN CENTRE
YARMOUTH, ISLE OF WIGHT

Like many good schemes, this modestly scaled design and call centre for a clothing firm was born out of adversity. A planning crisis – locally approved plans were called in by the Secretary of State – gave the client the opportunity to rethink and ask new architects to see what could be done with a set of cow sheds. The building had to be stylish and economical, and it had to be completed in a few months if the business was not to suffer. The Manser Practice suggested a construction management approach, so work started almost immediately, albeit 'at risk', while the planning and design processes took their course.

In design terms the result is imaginative and indeed extremely stylish, with black-stained timber cladding and a sheet-metal roof enclosing large interior volumes that look directly out over the countryside through floor-to-eaves glazing. The overall result is a delight and the project is a welcome demonstration of ambition in an area of high unemployment that is rarely chosen as a location for progressive companies.

In potentially unpromising circumstances, the architect has displayed the full value of creativity applied to existing structures, personal commitment and a complete understanding of the client's needs. This is backed up by the views of everyone from managing director: 'The building is a business statement rather than a fashion statement,' to the call centre manager: 'When you enter the building even on a sunny day, you don't mind because it's such a positive environment.'

CLIENTS Glynn and Claire Locke
STRUCTURAL ENGINEER Tari Williams Associates
M&E ENGINEER L Bishop & Partners

QS Colin Brookes
CONTRACTOR J Peck Construction
CONTRACT VALUE £1 million
PHOTOGRAPHY The Manser Practice

The Manser Practice

HOUSE AT JACOB'S LADDER
OXFORDSHIRE

Surprisingly, this is the first time this former Young Architect of the Year has won an RIBA Award; this year he has made up for lost time by winning two. The beautiful site, in mature woodland on an escarpment in the Chilterns, demanded an exceptional response; the judges agreed that this building gave one. The client took the view that the architecture should be a frame for its surroundings, not the other way round. In this respect too the architects have succeeded, producing an object that is beautiful but does not draw excessive attention to itself.

The planners had demanded a 'Chilterns-style' house, whatever that is, that had to match the exact footprint of the old, derelict house. Luckily, the same authority had previously authorised Chipperfield's Rowing Museum at Henley, so the architects were able to cite this timber-clad structure as an example of a modern building that echoed the vernacular without reiterating it. The tactic worked: the new plans went through unaltered.

With a lightness of touch evident in structure, materials and landscape, the house makes inventive use of the steep slope to create a series of unfolding spaces that defies the apparent regularity of its organisation. Largely transparent, the building's internal and external views are delightful and full of variety. Entering across a deck at first-floor level, glimpses of the countryside, suddenly withheld, draw you through the house. Descending into the living room, the full glory of the view is revealed. This journey ends with a sight line along a black tiled swimming pool. Diving in, you swim straight towards the view.

SOUTH

CLIENTS David and Shelley Grey

STRUCTURAL ENGINEER Price & Myers

M&E ENGINEER Michael Popper Associates

QS Sworn King and Partners

CONTRACT VALUE £412,000

PHOTOGRAPHY David Grey

Niall McLaughlin Architects

SAÏD BUSINESS SCHOOL, UNIVERSITY OF OXFORD

Rich benefactors do not always commission the best architecture, but as with the William Gates building in Cambridge, this donation has been put to good use. The school occupies an important city-centre site, very much town rather than gown. Since the closure of the old Midland station in the 1950s, the site opposite the rebuilt Western Region station was used as a car park. Arriving passengers now have a view of a building of substance and architectural quality, seen across a new public square. The scale and spatial sophistication of the project, its use of carefully detailed high-quality materials and its overtly architectural references, underline the client's ambition for a building that holds its own in the town, and with the historic colleges in particular.

The building retains a sense of unity through the use of a double-height cloister, following the Oxbridge precedent of creating largely inward-looking environments. This impressive architectural solution seems to have gained in conviction as the project evolved across two different sites. In terms of its townscape contribution, the cloister opens up towards the town square, creating a dramatic, canopied entrance. The copper spire, ostensibly to accommodate mechanical plant, is an entirely appropriate addition to the Oxford skyline. The architects have created a memorable building and served the client well over a long and difficult period.

CLIENT The Saïd Business School Foundation
STRUCTURAL ENGINEER Whitby Bird & Partners
M&E ENGINEER Whitby Bird & Partners

QS Gardiner & Theobald
CONTRACTOR Holloway White Allom
CONTRACT VALUE £25 million
PHOTOGRAPHY Dennis Gilbert/VIEW

Jeremy Dixon . Edward Jones

WHITELEY PRIMARY SCHOOL
FAREHAM, HAMPSHIRE

Whiteley is a new and fast-growing community, established in the mid 1980s. An earlier plan specified a new primary school for 420 with much-needed community facilities, but lack of a suitable site and a surge in numbers led to a decision to expand the existing school. The constraints of a limited budget, a fragile site crossed by a winter stream and a large water main, plus various changes of level, presented additional challenges. Here, in the latest in a long line of distinguished school buildings in Hampshire, the architects have fulfilled the brief and overcome the difficulties admirably.

Many of the familiar Colin Stansfield Smith-inspired ideas are in evidence here: the charming child-friendly internal spaces, the linear plan and circulation spine, the clever links with external spaces. Both staff and pupils are clearly delighted with these features, most of which are familiar from previous similar buildings.

Elsewhere, school design may be taking fresh directions (see the high-rise Hampden Gurney School in London), but Hampshire continues with its tried, tested and appropriate formula. It has set itself such high standards over the years that it is easy to underestimate the scale of the achievement here: compared to schools presently being procured by the PFI system elsewhere, this formula is a valuable benchmark.

CLIENT Hampshire County Council Education Committee
STRUCTURAL ENGINEER R J Watkinson
M&E ENGINEER Capita
QS Hampshire County Council
LANDSCAPING Anna Longley in association with Hampshire County Council Planning Dept
CONTRACTORS Ballast Wiltshier/Braziers
CONTRACT VALUE £3 million
PHOTOGRAPHY Paul Carter

Hampshire County Council Architects

BANDSTAND, DE LA WARR PAVILION
BEXHILL ON SEA

126

This tiny project manages to enhance the setting of one of the great buildings of the modern movement, Mendelsohn and Chermayeff's grade I-listed De La Warr Pavilion, itself the subject of a rolling programme of restoration led by John McAslan. The bandstand was an inspirational commission which involved community-wide consultation. School children, local people, client, contractors and consultants were all co-opted on to the design team. Six school projects on the subject were worked up as models by the architects and several of their ideas inform the built structure. Acoustic engineers and builder were also brought in at an early stage and made significant contributions to the design.

The form is exhilarating, recalling both the dynamics of early modernism and present day organic aspirations. The materials are quite simple – fibreglass on a plywood frame – the technology derives from the world of boat building. The shell shape is subject to wind loads of up to six times the weight of the structure, so it has to be braced and held down by a steel structure. Even so, it can be moved to different positions on the terrace to suit particular activities and weather conditions.

The jury was impressed both by the process and the end product, a highly useful, durable structure extending the activities around the pavilion. Architect and client have worked together with an admirable clarity of thought to achieve excellent results. The bandstand is a symbol of the cultural and social regeneration of a seaside town too often dismissed as merely a retirement haven.

Shortlisted for The Stephen Lawrence Prize.

SOUTH-EAST

CLIENT Rother District Council
STRUCTURAL ENGINEER Price & Myers
ACOUSTIC DESIGN Paul Gilleron

CONTRACTOR Westside Design Workshop
CONTRACT VALUE £54,000
PHOTOGRAPHY Niall McLaughlin

Niall McLaughlin Architects

KENT MESSENGER MILLENNIUM BRIDGE
MAIDSTONE

This is one of two bridges designed by the same architects and both generated by an ambitious project funded by the Millennium Commission, which has turned the banks of the Medway into a new 10-kilometre linear park. Landscape, architecture and public art are fused to excellent effect in this green oasis close to the traffic-clogged town centre.

The bridge was designed in collaboration with a world expert in stress-ribbon bridges. The system involves a deck made from precast concrete planks, resting on a set of cables. There is no need for bearings or expansion joints, so such structures can be light and have less environmental impact than conventional bridges. This is the world's first cranked stress-ribbon bridge, i.e. the first to change direction in mid-stream.

The sheer elegance of the structure and the regeneration context of the project dispelled any questions about the need for such complexity. The bridge, claimed as the cheapest millennium bridge in the UK, is a symbol of civic pride and reflects generous public and private funding. Its strong form, a deliberate objective in the project, makes an appropriate mark without dominating the scene. Construction is of excellent quality, with well-chosen components which should ensure safety and durability.

Architect and engineer have worked with the client to make something of memorable beauty, involving a range of crafts and skills. This bridge alone makes a visit to Maidstone well worthwhile.

CLIENT Maidstone Borough Council
STRUCTURAL ENGINEER Strasky Husty & Partners
SITE ENGINEER Lewin Fryer & Partners

QS AYH
CONTRACTOR Balfour Beatty
CONTRACT VALUE £900,000
PHOTOGRAPHY Cezary Bednarski

Cezary Bednarski with Studio E Architects

THE LODGE, WHITHURST PARK
WEST SUSSEX

This is a subtle and finely crafted private house, which enhances its beautiful parkland setting without suburbanising it. It was achieved only after a successful appeal against the refusal of planning consent. Not far away, another house, a weak pastiche of the Tudor style, is under construction. It gained planning approval without dispute.

The 40-hectare park in which the house sits includes an oak wood and pasture; part of it is owned by the National Trust. The architect was challenged by an informed client to produce a response to this context that was both contemporary and appropriate. He has done so without any resort to literal historicism or the more obvious vernacular references (though there are arts and crafts, and even Shaker, undertones). The architect was inspired by the form of the steep pitched hay barn, open at ground-floor level. From a distance, the house might be mistaken for a barn, yet it makes no attempt to disguise its function. The interior has real drama, but this has not been achieved at the expense of practicality. The living spaces are comfortable and enjoyable; the largely timber-framed first floor has a special quality of delight.

Client, architect and contractor worked closely together to achieve a finished product of high quality – the craftsmanship is in tune with the fine materials, including quantities of untreated English oak, zinc and fair-faced concrete, materials that combine to make up a quasi-agricultural aesthetic. The building has integrity, consistency and conviction and could be an inspiration to mass builders working in the region.

CLIENTS Richard Taylor and Rick Englert
STRUCTURAL ENGINEER Alan Conisbee & Associates
QS Holden Associates

CONTRACTOR Ceecom Ltd
CONTRACT VALUE £486,000
PHOTOGRAPHY David Churchill

James Gorst Architects

PFIZER HEADQUARTERS
TADWORTH, SURREY

International pharmaceutical company Pfizer decided in 1998 to move its administrative and sales staff to Tadworth from East Kent. The parkland site had been occupied by an undistinguished country house but contained fine trees and other features worth retaining. The new building (completed in two phases – the award is for phase I) was designed to a client brief that demanded interactive spaces for team-working and creative thought alongside more conventional offices. The centre of the building is an internal top-lit street, well furnished and adorned with works of art, from where fingers of office space extend on three levels. Large areas are given over to meeting and social space.

This is a building in the best hi-tech tradition, with details – internal bridges, for example – which evoke a nautical and industrial image and can occasionally seem heavy handed. Furnishing and fit-out have been overseen by the architects, to excellent effect. The precise and elegant detailing of the exterior is admirable. Even the bicycle sheds have been subjected to a thoughtful design process – here they are truly architecture. The overall result is of a luminous and spacious workplace which has entirely met the demands of the brief.

The building sits serenely in its green setting, which enhances the employee's working experience – it seems to be highly popular with staff. The jury felt that this was an exceptionally good piece of commercial architecture and that its conviction and commitment to quality should be firmly encouraged.

STRUCTURAL ENGINEER Arup

M&E ENGINEER Arup

QS Franklin & Andrews

LANDSCAPE ARCHITECT Derek Lovejoy Partnership

CONTRACTOR Laing Ltd

CONTRACT VALUE £39 million

PHOTOGRAPHY Morley von Sternberg

Sheppard Robson

SOUTH-EAST

SORREL HOUSE
BOSHAM HOE, WEST SUSSEX

The Sorrel House was designed by the late Peter Foggo and David Thomas in 1960, when both were employed by Architects' Co-Partnership. It has been described as a 'supreme example' of the taste for timber building of that period. The historian Elain Harwood has written: 'The whole gives the impression of being created from a kit of parts, a conceit rarely realised elsewhere.' The house was listed grade II* in 1998.

David Thomas has overseen two phases of expansion; in the 1970s, when the building lost its original symmetry and, more recently, a final phase which has restored it. In the process, the house has been adapted to present-day lifestyles. Built as a weekend house by a creek, it is currently a permanent home for a young family. The jury was captivated by this building, by its lightness of touch, its fine craftsmanship with something of a boat-building aesthetic, and the exhilaration of being raised up on stilts above the estuary. The jury questioned whether the extension should have reflected the style of today, but decided this was impossible to define. Both phases of extension are seamless and constructed to the standard of the original.

This is a good example of the updating of an historic building and the clients are to be commended for their continuing collaboration with the original architect. Although the award is given for the most recent work, it is also a belated recognition by the RIBA of the distinction of Foggo and Thomas' work of 1960.

Shortlisted for The Crown Estate Conservation Award and The Stephen Lawrence Prize.

SOUTH-EAST

CLIENT George W Scott
STRUCTURAL ENGINEER Foggo Associates
M&E ENGINEER Foggo Associates

QS Foggo Associates
CONTRACTOR John C Lillywhite
CONTRACT VALUE £79,000
PHOTOGRAPHY Peter Mackinven

Foggo Associates, in association with David Thomas

BROOKE COOMBES HOUSE
EALING

The Brooke Coombes House, set within a suburban conservation area in Ealing, won the 2002 Manser Medal for one-off houses. It was a project that was not limited by commonly understood 'self-build' methods or construction materials.

The house demonstrates a mature attitude to space and integral living, placing the living accommodation in one strip and dividing the main areas with freestanding pods housing worktop or fireplace. Also running the full depth of the house is a double-height glazed courtyard space, forming a buffer zone and means of passive solar collection and allowing the rest of the house to be very open. A water channel runs through it, and around the house, feeding ponds in the gardens and helping to integrate the garden and house. The undercroft, beneath the house, provides a cool storage area and a cool air reservoir for the water channel. On the upper floor, a glazed strip between wall and roof allows light into the bedrooms and views out over the treetops.

This building is a creative and sustainable building design and also a reflection of its owners' way of life. Despite the tight plan – almost half of the footprint is occupied by the conservatory – there is no sense of feeling cramped and every room benefits from light from two sides. The jury was at pains to congratulate the architects on giving the owners a home they are delighted with.

Shortlisted for the AJ First Building Award.

CLIENTS John Brooke and Carol Coombes
STRUCTURAL ENGINEER Elliott Wood Partnership
M&E ENGINEER Max Fordham & Partners
QS Moulton Taggart
CONTRACTOR self-build
CONTRACT VALUE £300,000
PHOTOGRAPHY Charlotte Wood

LONDON

Burd Haward Marston Architects

FAIRHAZEL GARDENS
LONDON NW6

The architects have used this project as a laboratory to try out new ideas and techniques. Set within a conservation area of Victorian red-brick mansion blocks, this new house and studio for the architects draws from the palate of surrounding materials to create a building that is clearly contemporary yet comfortable with its older neighbours. Built to a relatively tight budget, it uses a modular construction, exploiting standard material sizes and a simple constructional form for economy.

The two-bedroom house maintains the size of an earlier planning permission for the site and takes the form of two simple boxes, the larger with living, sleeping and working areas on the ground floor, and the smaller containing the bedrooms above. The two-storey element sits to the front of the long narrow site, relating to the scale and building line of the adjacent houses, but steps down towards the garden at the rear and a meadow beyond. The steel-framed house is infilled along its sides by a combination of brick, timber and etched glass panels for privacy. The ends of the frame are glazed with floor-to-ceiling panels, flooding the interior with daylight. On the upper floor the bedrooms are screened from the street by a brick plane balanced above the huge glass window to the studio below. The garden side is fully glazed, looking out over a flat roof planted with a mat of heathers and moss that changes colour through the seasons.

The design is handled in an assured and elegant manner that employs an Eames-like modular language to create a thoughtful and enjoyable family house.
Shortlisted for the AJ First Building Award and for The Stephen Lawrence Prize.

CLIENTS Mr and Mrs A Barnett
STRUCTURAL ENGINEER Arup
M&E ENGINEER Arup

CONTRACTORS various
CONTRACT VALUE £180,000
PHOTOGRAPHY Paul Tyagi

Scampton + Barnett

HOUSE IN ARTHUR ROAD
WIMBLEDON

To build a house on a site just five metres wide and 80 metres long is one challenge, to do it in as significant a location as the ridge that runs across Wimbledon is another. The architects have responded by building vertically, producing a prominent local marker.

The house is a concrete substructure with timber-framed, oak-clad tower and the steel-framed rear section in engineering brick. The different materials define the three areas of the house: sleeping, stairway, and living. These simple interlocked volumes reflect the internal planning and programme of the building. Sleeping accommodation is in the tower, which sits on a concrete base; a brick cube contains the stair; and the area under the planted vaulted roof has the living spaces. The interior plays with the perception of space, compressing then opening out to create a sequence of changing and ambiguous volumes. Internal finishes are white walls with oak and black slate floors. Elements of the in-situ concrete are exposed on the main staircase; the same material used for a table defines a boundary between living and kitchen areas.

The house is unashamedly modern, with an honest use of materials and plain detailing. The architect showed determination in obtaining planning permission and, having won it, made creative use of the tight site and modest budget. Modern builders of the terraced house can definitely learn from this one.

LONDON

CLIENT Terry Pawson
STRUCTURAL ENGINEER Barton Engineers

CONTRACTOR various
CONTRACT VALUE £310,000
PHOTOGRAPHY Richard Bryant/ARCAID

Terry Pawson Architects

IROKO HOUSING CO-OPERATIVE
UPPER GROUND

Coin Street are genuinely community builders: for them homes do not exist in isolation but as part of a social framework of education, sports and community amenities, linking into the wider city with its transport, cultural and employment facilities.

Formerly occupied by several large warehouses, the site was cleared to basement level over ten years ago and then used as a car park. The brief called for some of the site to be retained for public parking – the new car park is below ground and the housing was developed from ground floor upwards. Of the 59 dwellings, 32 are family houses with the balance made up of a mix of flats and maisonettes. The remaining 30 per cent of the site area is reserved for a community facilities building.

Each dwelling has two elevations: the public streetscape expressed in brick, and the private timber-clad façade overlooking the landscaped garden space. Otherwise there is no formal 'front' and 'rear' to the dwellings. The solar panels on the roof provide hot water, reducing living expenses for the occupants. Each dwelling is fitted with mechanical background ventilation offering residents maximum comfort control.

The co-operative is non profit-making, any surpluses go back into the housing, lowering management costs and rents. This system also provides on-site management so that the usual problems of high-density social housing, such as the supervision of communal spaces, lifts and stairs, can be adequately controlled.

Coin Street Community Builders were shortlisted for the RIBA Client of the Year Award.

LONDON

CLIENT Coin Street Community Builders
STRUCTURAL ENGINEER Price & Myers
M&E ENGINEER Atelier Ten
QS Davis Langdon & Everest

CONTRACTOR Mansell plc
CONTRACT VALUE £12 million
PHOTOGRAPHY Peter Durant

Haworth Tompkins Architects

KEELING HOUSE
CLAREDALE STREET, BETHNAL GREEN

A neat summation of the architectural-cum-social history of the second half of the twentieth century is contained in this project. Denys Lasdun's four residential towers, built in 1956 on a bomb site, had fallen out of fashion and into disrepair. Tower Hamlets Council was forced to empty the blocks and seal off the site to prevent further vandalism to the listed structures. Having failed to interest any housing association in them, they sold the blocks off to private developers with an eye on the lucrative apartment market.

The architects collaborated closely with Lasdun in his last years and with English Heritage to return Keeling House to its original condition and colours as far as possible. They also addressed areas of the design which had not worked, increasing safety and security throughout the open deck-access levels, creating a new entrance area and the surrounding landscape to enclose and manage access to the central lift core.

The elegant new entrance pavilion is shaped by the strong geometry of the angled towers. The new landscaping and pool create a secure perimeter around their base and draw upon the sculpted language of the concrete, emphasising the lightness of the aluminium wing roof, which apparently hovers over the new entrance space. The crispness of the new elements is carried through in the detailing of the glass, stone and aluminium which are used to form the new elements: a language which derives from the practice's Mount Stuart visitors centre project on the Isle of Bute.

CLIENT Lincoln Holdings
STRUCTURAL ENGINEER Anthony Hunt Associates
LANDSCAPE ARCHITECT Gillespies

CONTRACTOR Lincoln Holdings Construction Management
CONTRACT VALUE £2.5 million
PHOTOGRAPHY Richard Bryant/ARCAID

Munkenbeck + Marshall

NEW PYM HOUSE, ANGELL TOWN
BRIXTON

The aim of this community housing scheme was to reintegrate the estate into the surrounding area of Brixton. Seventy new dwellings have been designed, fronting a series of new streets, mews and open spaces. In addition, an outdoor sports area integrates well with the dwellings and their individual gardens. Careful attention has been paid to layout of spaces and details of each element of construction. Each dwelling has an individual identity, and front entrances are limited to a maximum of two households sharing.

The architecture is exemplary in many ways, but especially in the delightful quality of the environment that has been created. The urban design objectives were achieved by re-inscribing a street layout; establishing an active public realm at ground-floor level and a hierarchy of public and private space; deinstitutionalising the estate; creating safe routes for people who use and live on the estate; and solving related problems of security, refuse, parking and generally hostile surroundings.

This is an exemplary social housing development; a triumph for stakeholder power and the programmes that support them. There is a generosity of space and detail that most private developers would be jealous of: floor-to-floor glazing, balconies and even condensing boilers. The development is dense but low-rise, showing that height is not the only answer to density. There was extensive community consultation and the residents took an active role in design and construction, and now in maintenance and security.

LONDON

CLIENT London Borough of Lambeth
STRUCTURAL ENGINEER Adams Kara Taylor
M&E ENGINEER Monal Associates

QS Dobson White Boulcott
CONTRACTOR Higgins Construction plc
CONTRACT VALUE £6 million
PHOTOGRAPHY Morley von Sternberg

Burrell Foley Fischer LLP

ROYAL ACADEMY OF MUSIC
MARYLEBONE ROAD

The project is on one of the most challenging sites in the capital yet still manages to insert a piece of modern architecture capable of holding its own against the surrounding Nash and Hardwick buildings. The grade I-listed York Gate building by John Nash was purchased in 1997 by the Royal Academy of Music, and now provides teaching, rehearsal, museum and archive spaces.

As much of the interior of York Gate post-dates its original façades, the architects were able to carry out extensive reworking, resulting in two densely packed banks of practice rooms, offices and archives, arranged around a central corridor on each floor. Glazed slots allow glimpses into the rooms and daylight into the corridor, while its crisply detailed white finishes with their bold graphics create a surprisingly modern, ship-like feel within the shell of the nineteenth-century building. While the sounds of practising are allowed to spill out, the practice rooms are acoustically isolated from one another to prevent interference.

Planning restrictions demanded that the York Gate building and the original Marylebone Street building be kept visually separate, so a new subterranean area has been created linking the two. An etched glass ceiling floods these spaces with daylight. At the heart of this link is a new concert hall that can be used by an 80-piece orchestra and shows itself above ground as an elegant zinc-clad barrel vault.

Shortlisted for the ADAPT Trust Access Award.

STRUCTURAL ENGINEER Oscar Faber
M&E ENGINEER Oscar Faber
QS Gardiner & Theobald
ACOUSTICS ENGINEER Sandy Brown
Associates

ACCESS CONSULTANT David Bonnett
CONTRACTOR Simons Interiors London
CONTRACT VALUE £6 million
PHOTOGRAPHY Peter Cook/VIEW

John McAslan & Partners

SOUTHWARK CATHEDRAL MILLENNIUM PROJECT
LONDON SE1

Southwark Cathedral enjoys – if that is the right word – one of the tightest sites of any cathedral in the country. The brief called for the cathedral's position as the spiritual focus of the South Bank to be emphasised more strongly; for increased access for disabled visitors; for a new entrance for people who approach from the riverside walk to the north; and for new ancillary accommodation, including a refectory, shop and theological library.

A new linking 'street', with a shop at ground level, runs parallel to the cathedral, extending into a new exhibition located within the existing building. The new buildings are of limestone and Norfolk flint, with a Westmoreland slate roof with copper detailing – all materials that tie the new and the old work together. Initially traditional in appearance, the stonework in fact conceals a contemporary structural system of precast concrete beams and vaults in the ground-floor refectory and structural ribs in the library above.

The new buildings create a series of spaces that respect and gain inspiration from the historic context. Development of the site skilfully links the new buildings with the cathedral, providing a new tourist attraction while maintaining the calm and sanctity of the religious site itself. The project was officially opened by Nelson Mandela in May 2001. Also shortlisted for the ADAPT Trust Access Award.

LONDON

CLIENTS The Very Reverend Colin Slee and the Cathedral Church of St Saviour and St Mary Overie Southwark
STRUCTURAL ENGINEER Alan Baxter & Associates
M&E ENGINEER Max Fordham LLP

QS Citex
LANDSCAPE ARCHITECT Elizabeth Banks Associates
CONTRACTOR Walter Lilly & Co Ltd
CONTRACT VALUE £10 million
PHOTOGRAPHY Dennis Gilbert/VIEW

Richard Griffiths Architects

TALKBACK PRODUCTIONS
NEWMAN STREET

Creative companies do not always make for creative clients, but Talkback Productions are the exception that proves the rule. The architects have produced a truly democratic building that allows production teams and clients to interact, with few physical signs of hierarchy. This scheme combines the integration of the existing façades in Newman Street and Newman Passage with the insertion of a new two-storey building between them.

The building has been constructed to provide each production team with a 'front door'. The upper-floor workspaces are light, airy and colourful and are designed to invigorate their occupants, while the common room, adjoining servery kitchen, meeting rooms and offices located on the ground floor, are glazed with vents for natural ventilation. The studio, edit suites, green room and plant are situated in the basement.

Terraces and decks, bridges and courts provide a variety of circulation routes, meetings places and relaxation areas. There are two gardens on the first-floor level; a herb garden and a lawn. Environmental design underpins the scheme, which incorporates natural ventilation, night-time cooling and solar shading provided by the decks and zinc cowls. Water collected from the roofs is stored in the basement and used to water the garden.

With the creation of a unique internal courtyard that optimises the use of sun, daylighting and natural ventilation, this feels like an oasis away from the chaos of Oxford Street.

STRUCTURAL ENGINEER Dewhurst Macfarlane & Partners
M&E ENGINEER Fulcrum Consulting
LANDSCAPE ARCHITECT Jones Environmental

QS BPTW
CONTRACTOR Higgins City Ltd
CONTRACT VALUE £2.4 million
PHOTOGRAPHY Nick Kane

LONDON

Buschow Henley Architects

TATE BRITAIN CENTENARY DEVELOPMENT
MILLBANK

The Tate was keen to maximise visitor numbers, inevitably affected by the opening of Tate Modern. The centenary development was designed as a seamless connection between the new building and the existing grade II*-listed building. The major requirements of the project were to provide a new public entrance off Atterbury Street and a new shop; to create six galleries and refurbish nine existing ones; and to upgrade services. Construction took three years, and included excavating seven metres beneath the new building. It was financed by the Heritage Lottery Fund and private donations.

The new Manton entrance provides a major alternative with disabled access to the existing stepped entrance in Millbank. This design work was done by Allford Hall Monaghan Morris. As visitors enter, the focal point is the welcoming red wall of the information desk, behind a curved glass podium. The new galleries are reached by the new staircase or lift (big enough to transport large pieces of art). Fibrous plaster-vaulted ceilings allow for greater visual height in the exhibition galleries with suspended uplighters underneath. A glazed slot in the northwest wall of the perimeter gallery allows visitors to orientate themselves and brings some daylight into the exhibition space. This is a magnificent and accomplished intervention to the existing landmark building.

Shortlisted for the ADAPT Trust Access Award and The Crown Estate Conservation Award. The Tate was additionally shortlisted for The RIBA Client of the Year Award.

CLIENT The Directors and Trustees of the Tate Gallery
STRUCTURAL ENGINEER Campbell Reith Hill
M&E ENGINEER SVM

QS Turner & Townsend
LANDSCAPE ARCHITECT Allies & Morrison
CONTRACTOR Mace
CONTRACT VALUE £22 million
PHOTOGRAPHY Richard Bryant/ARCAID

John Miller + Partners

VXO HOUSE
HAMPSTEAD

Don't be put off by the V sign that greets you on arrival – stick with it and you'll be in for an architectural treat that harks back to pop art days. This radical reworking of a 1960s house reveals a series of structures, linked by the use of steel structural letters: 'V' (house), 'X' (gym/guest room) and 'O' (car-port). Like a lot of good architecture, there was an element of chance to it. A fire seriously damaged the original house and its 1970s extensions. Alison Brooks has seized the opportunity, scooping an atrium out of the heart of the house, letting in light and framing views of Hampstead.

The client, who worked with the architect when she was at Ron Arad's, was looking for a way to reconfigure the house interior and create a generous entrance hall and an additional bedroom. The solution involves cutting large openings in the cross walls to connect living spaces horizontally, vertically and to the garden, allowing as much natural light as possible to penetrate the house. Brooks has also reworked the first floor so all the bedrooms look out on to a central hall and a new double-height gallery (where there once was an inaccessible roof terrace). All the windows have been replaced to match the light aluminium-framed new glazing. Barnet Council's conservation office is to be commended for insisting that the new work maintained the stepping back composition of the original 1960s house.
Shortlisted for the AJ First Building Award.

CLIENT private
STRUCTURAL ENGINEER Price & Myers
CONTRACTOR Italmaster

CONTRACT VALUE £587,000
PHOTOGRAPHY Dennis Gilbert/VIEW

Alison Brooks Architects

BRAUN EUROPEAN HEADQUARTERS

MELSUNGEN, GERMANY

Braun, the international medical and electrical suppliers, asked Michael Wilford to design the latest phase of their European headquarters in the beautiful wooded Fulda valley near Melsungen. The site had previously been developed between 1987 and 1992 to a James Stirling masterplan, by Stirling himself, with Michael Wilford and Walter Näegli. The original buildings and landscape have matured well and are a formidable act to follow. That the outcome is excellent in its own right, while paying self-confident respect to the established architectural order, is a tribute to the whole design team.

The new building sits next to the existing administration block and points arrow-like towards the original factory. A three-storey triangular office building sits atop a two-storey drum containing technical facilities. The deep-set windows recall those of the earlier building. A lightwell penetrates all these volumes; its exposed concrete drum expressed throughout the offices. An enclosed bridge links the new and old administration blocks. Construction and detailing is of the highest order throughout. The relief and depth of the façades, emphasised by the use of contrasting colours and materials, is echoed in the sculptural interplay of the building's toy-like forms.

The offices use a hot-desking system developed by Braun's chairman which reduces the workstation requirement of 25 square metres per employee to 13 square metres. A refurbished staff restaurant in one of the old blocks enjoys remarkable views. In all, this is a complex that it is a privilege to visit and must be even more of one to work in.

CLIENT B Braun Melsungen AG
STRUCTURAL ENGINEER Ing. Büro Dr Meyer
M&E ENGINEER ROM

CONTRACTOR Dyckerhoff & Widmann AG
COST €11 million
PHOTOGRAPHY Roland Halbe

Michael Wilford & Partners

BURDA MEDIEN PARK
OFFENBURG, GERMANY

This is a very good example of an elegant, low density, high-quality but simple office for the 600 staff of the Burda Publishing Company, built in an unremarkable suburb of Offenburg. Often German office buildings can be gloomy inside because of rigorous environmental standards. Here, there is a generosity of space throughout, in foyer, corridors and offices and the deceptively simple plan of a curving spine with six wings admits light to every corner and curve, using it playfully in the created shadows, as well as practically. This is a building which adds up well in three dimensions – and does not compromise on its green credentials.

The offices are on four tiered levels in each wing under a gently curving concrete roof form that meets the ground, shielding the interior from both noise and solar gain. The slab includes chilled water and is part of a sensible and efficient environmental control package. The spaces between the wings provide a sheltered and landscaped micro-climate for all workers to look out on to and use.

Tables and chairs are provided on the grass for al fresco meetings. Internal meeting rooms facing the street help to animate an otherwise less interesting elevation. This is not a building that attempts anything particularly new, yet the whole is more than the sum of the parts, and it is all of a standard that would be the envy of most British workers.

CLIENT Hubert Burda Media
STRUCTURAL ENGINEER Werner Sobek Ingenieure
M&E ENGINEERS HL-Technik AG/ Orfgens + Partner
LANDSCAPE ARCHITECT Weber Klein Maas Landschaftsarchitekten
CONTRACTOR Ingenhoven Overdiek Planungsgesellschaft GmbH
COST DM55 million
PHOTOGRAPHY H G Esch

Ingenhoven Overdiek Kahlen und Partner

EXPERIMENTAL FACTORY
MAGDEBURG, GERMANY

In a far from colourful eastern German town, sauerbruch hutton have pulled off another of their totemic buildings: a multifunctional and interdisciplinary research factory – a building that will facilitate fast and efficient production and marketing of products – that brings together the private and university sectors.

The experimental factory sits in a dreary campus and brightens it up with the practice's signature use of colour. Here, they have courageously draped a striped blanket of coloured aluminium over three very different scales of space and given them a coherence. The east and west façades are formed by the ends of the blanket, tucked in where it meets the ground. The north and south faces are cut away and clad in translucent glass. Inside are 3400 square metres of space for laboratories, testing halls, offices and lecture halls: research, development and prototype production all under one remarkable roof. The cladding gives the building good thermal performance and protects it from traffic noise.

Externally colour embodies the idea of renewal and reinvigoration of a rather down-at-heel campus; internally its use is just as beautifully conceived and executed. A double-height foyer employs colour to enliven what could be a rather dead space. A generous gallery overlooking the foyer establishes visual connections between the areas and functions.

EUROPEAN UNION

CLIENT Zentrum für Produkt Verfahrens und Processinnovations GmbH
STRUCTURAL ENGINEER Bautra
ENVIRONMENTAL ENGINEER Canzler Ingenieure

QS Harms and Partner
CONTRACTOR Oeverman GmbH & Co
COST £5 million
PHOTOGRAPHY Gerrit Engel

sauerbruch hutton architects

FINGAL COUNTY OFFICES
SWORDS, CO. DUBLIN, IRELAND

New public buildings generally fall into one of two extreme categories: either lottery funded arts projects or the almost universally uninspired design-build PFI solutions. Most buildings for local authorities fit the latter category, but Fingal County offices are a triumphant exception to any such generalisation.

Fingal County is a new authority which set out, through an open competition, to commission new headquarters as an expression of democratic local government, and to house 450 employees, including its own planners and architects. This is the result of a marriage between the young practice of Bucholz McEvoy, whose first building this is, and the Dublin office of Building Design Partnership, who acted as project architects.

Three five-storey wings of shallow, cross-ventilated offices are linked across one end by a stunning vertical main street, the outside entrance wall of which is a full height curved structural glass screen inspired by Peter Rice. At one end is the circular council chamber, a light and airy space, open along one wall to the gaze of passers-by outside.

Great efforts have been made to achieve a sustainable, low-energy building and the entire building is naturally ventilated. A combination of curved precast concrete ceilings, integrated lighting and a curtain wall providing natural opening lights and solar shading obviates any need for artificial cooling in the shallow-plan offices.

These offices at once raise the status of a small town, modest in its civic character, to that of an appropriate seat of local government.

Shortlisted for The RIBA Journal Sustainability Award.

CLIENT Fingal County Council	**GLASS WALL ENGINEER** RFR Paris
STRUCTURAL ENGINEER Arup	**CONTRACTOR** P J Hegarty & Son
M&E ENGINEER BDP	**COST** £9 million
QS Boyd & Creed	**PHOTOGRAPHY** Michael Moran

Bucholz McEvoy in association with BDP Dublin

FRANKFURT MESSEHALLE
GERMANY

Here Grimshaw's have used their ability to see the big picture to remarkable effect. The volumes of the new Messehalle, commissioned in 2000 following an international competition, are simply stunning. The complex, laid out over two massive storeys, creates 40,000 square metres of exhibition space, fed by twin blocks of four-storey foyer access. With visitor numbers of up to 120,000 per day, pedestrian tours create conditions akin to major urban transport interchanges, with which Grimshaw's are of course very familiar.

As at Waterloo International Station, it is the roof – a single folded-plate structure formed from a continuous network of welded steel tubes spanning 165 metres – that makes the project extraordinary. The services, acoustic and lighting are integrated within the massive spans and manifest in the service bridges that are suspended delicately from the structure. Clerestory glazing draws light deep inside the building. The lower hall, lacking the same drama, still impresses. This single volume is probably better than any other exhibition space in Germany.

The design of the building has been conceived creatively and courageously from concept to detail, pared back to its essentials and is strikingly efficient and cost effective. Its assembly in 16 months by a construction team of 700, with a massive monthly spend, is a tribute to the project team and to the whole German construction industry. Not for the first time on such a trip, the judges remarked, 'Why can't we do this in the UK?'

ASSOCIATE ARCHITECT ABB
STRUCTURAL ENGINEERS Arup GmbH/
Schlaich Bergermann/BGS/Hahn
Bartenbach
M&E ENGINEERS Kuehn Bauer &
Partners/HL Technik/Dörflinger

QS Davis Langdon & Everest
CONTRACTORS Hochtief/Bilfinger +
Berger
COST DM270 million
PHOTOGRAPHY Waltraud Krase/Foto
Design

Nicholas Grimshaw and Partners

ASSESSORS

The RIBA is extremely grateful to the assessors – architects and non-architects – all of whom give their time freely.

THE STIRLING PRIZE JURY 2002
Paul Hyett – RIBA President (Chair), Paul Finch (sponsor and Editorial Director of *The Architects' Journal*), Wayne Hemingway (designer), Kate Mosse (novelist), Farshid Moussavi (Foreign Office Architects)

THE RIBA AWARDS GROUP JUDGES 2002
Ian Davidson (Chair), Tony Chapman, Stephen Hodder, Sir Peter Mason, Eric Parry, Jeremy Till, Joanna van Heyningen, Giles Worsley

REGIONAL ASSESSORS – RIBA AWARDS 2002
The judges are listed in the following order: chair of jury (nationally appointed architect); lay juror (non architect); regional representative (architect from region)
SCOTLAND Bob Allies; Ron Joiner; Alan Naylor
NORTHERN IRELAND David Page; Rory Coonan; Clyde Markwell
NORTH Jeffrey Bell; Lucy Musgrave; Peter Beacock
NORTH WEST Niall McLaughlin; Murray Grigor; Roger Haigh
YORKSHIRE Jeffrey Bell; Lucy Musgrave; John Edmonds
WALES Peter Clegg; Bob Ayling; Richard Woods
WEST MIDLANDS Julia Barfield; Richard Bryant; Angus Jamieson
EAST MIDLANDS Julia Barfield; Richard Bryant; Doug Sutherland
EAST Michael Fletcher; Alan Cherry; Peter Goodwin
SOUTH WEST Ian Simpson; Kevin McCloud; Louis Hawkins

WESSEX Ian Simpson; Kevin McCloud; Mark Ellerby

SOUTH Rab Bennetts; Jane Priestman; David Gregory

SOUTH EAST Pankaj Patel; Ken Powell; Mike Lawless

LONDON AREA 1 Gareth Hoskins; Tom Bloxham; Guy Greenfield

LONDON AREA 2 John McAslan; Guy Battle; Walter Menteth

EUROPE Ian Davidson; Stephen Hodder; David Levitt; Eric Parry; Jeremy Till; Joanna van Heyningen (architects)/Tony Chapman; Giles Worsley (lay assessors)

RIBA PRIZE WINNERS

STIRLING PRIZE

1996	Hodder Associates	The Centenary Building, University of Salford
1997	Sir James Stirling and Michael Wilford & Partners	The Music School, Stuttgart
1998	Foster & Partners	American Air Museum, Duxford
1999	Future Systems	NatWest Media Centre, Lord's, London
2000	Alsop & Störmer	Peckham Library & Media Centre
2001	Wilkinson Eyre Architects	Magna, Rotherham

THE STEPHEN LAWRENCE PRIZE

1998	Ian Ritchie Architects	Terrasson Cultural Greenhouse, France
1999	Munkenbeck + Marshall	Sculpture Gallery, Roche Court
2000	Softroom Architects	Kielder Belvedere
2001	Richard Rose-Casemore	Hatherley Studio, Winchester

THE CROWN ESTATE CONSERVATION AWARD

1998	Peter Inskip & Peter Jenkins	Temple of Concord and Victory, Stowe
1999	Foster & Partners	The Reichstag, Berlin, Germany
2000	Foster & Partners	JC Decaux UK Headquarters, London
2001	Rick Mather Architects	The Dulwich Picture Gallery

THE AJ FIRST BUILDING AWARD

In association with Robin Ellis Design Build

2001	Walker Architecture	Cedar House, Logiealmond

THE ADAPT TRUST ACCESS AWARD

2001   Avery Associates Architects   Royal Academy of Dramatic Arts, London

THE RIBA JOURNAL SUSTAINABILITY AWARD

2000   Chetwood Associates, Sainsbury's, Greenwich

2001   Michael Hopkins and Partners, Jubilee Campus, Nottingham University

RIBA CLIENT OF THE YEAR

In association with the Arts Council of England

1998   Roland Paoletti

1999   The MCC

2000   The Foreign & Commonwealth Office

2001   Molendinar Park Housing Association, Glasgow

SPONSORS

The RIBA is grateful to all the sponsors who make the awards possible, in particular *The Architects' Journal*, published by EMAP, our main sponsors, who provide the money for the Stirling Prize and its judging costs. *The Architects' Journal* also sponsors the AJ First Building Award with Robin Ellis Design Build. We are grateful for the continuing support of the ADAPT Trust, sponsors of the ADAPT Trust Access Award, *The RIBA Journal*, sponsors of the RIBA Journal Sustainability Award; the Arts Council of England for the RIBA Client of the Year; the Marco Goldschmied Foundation for The Stephen Lawrence Prize; and the Crown Estate, sponsors of the Conservation Award.

Once again this book, *Architecture 02*, is sponsored by Service Point digital reprographics and communications.

All RIBA Award winners receive a lead plaque which is placed on the building. The RIBA is grateful for the generous support of the Lead Sheet Association in manufacturing and presenting these plaques.

Finally, our thanks to The American Hardwood Export Council, Cous Colors, Kalzip, Montagu Evans, SIV Architectural Career Management and to Newcastle-Gateshead, joint bidders for European Capital of Culture in 2008, for their major contributions to the costs of the Stirling Prize event.

We are also grateful to Channel 4 for their continuing coverage of The RIBA Stirling Prize in association with *The Architects' Journal*.

THE STEPHEN LAWRENCE TRUST

The Stephen Lawrence Trust is a non-sectarian, non-political and non-profit-making body that aims to provide young black people with the opportunity to reach the goal Stephen was so cruelly denied, by encouraging students to apply to study architecture in the UK, in the Caribbean and in South Africa. The Lawrence family hopes that, in this way, architecture and its study will come to reflect more closely the culturally diverse communities living in and using it. The Trust is pledged to play a role in the improvement of community relations and hopes to stage an annual keynote lecture raising the profile of developments in race relations and architecture.

To find out more about the Trust (Charity registration No. 1070860) please write c/o Arthur Timothy Associates, St John's Hall, 9 Fair Street, London SE1 2XA, or phone 020 7387 9465, fax 020 7357 8079.

Digital Reprographics
Document Management
Facilities Management

SERVICE POINT

'Service Point have supported the Awards book since its launch back in 1998 and over that time it has become an essential part of the RIBA's programme. It has succeeded in bringing the winning buildings before an ever-wider public and encouraged people to get much more involved in the built environment. The RIBA is hugely indebted to Service Point for making the book possible once again.' Tony Chapman, Head of Awards at the Royal Institute of British Architects.

Service Point, the world's leading provider of Digital Reprographics, Document Management and Facilities Management to the Architecture, Engineering and Construction industries (a/e/c), take great pleasure in printing and presenting this year's Awards book in full colour and a new size, adding new dimensions not used before for these unique and impressive projects.

Service Point was a key supporter of Glasgow 1999. Likewise in Manchester they were closely involved in major urban redevelopment, extending support of a/e/c via sponsorship of the CUBE Gallery – the Centre for the Understanding of the Built Environment. Service Point continue to support the very community that supports its organisation for the mutual benefits of setting industry standards in design to build.

www.servicepointuk.com

SERVICE POINT

Some promise it ... Service Point deliver it ...

Service Point can provide a range of innovative solutions that no other reprographics company can, to completely digitise the document process allowing: reduction in archiving space, reduced risk of lost or damaged documents, full back-up on project completion and overall improvement in the management process ...

... the net results being reduced project completion times and increased profit margins.

Visit: www.servicepointuk.com
Or Freecall 0800 634 24 24

Service Point ... New Image ... New Services ... Helping you create New Horizons

Digital Reprographics
Document Management
Facilities Management